Dr. Rogal. FRANK

CONTENTS

Acknowledgments...ix
Foreword.. x
1. The New, Militant Atheism 1
2. What is Religion? 11
3. Did Science Disprove God? 21
4. Is There Evidence of God? 49
5. Is Christianity Intolerant? 73
6. Does Evil Disprove God?... 89
7. Are Moral Absolutes Real? 99
8. Are Miracles Possible? 107
9. What do Christians Believe?... 113
10. Is the New Testament Historically Reliable? 123
11. Did Jesus Really Claim to be God? 131
12. Did Jesus Really Rise from the Dead? 147
13. Is Teaching Children about God Child Abuse?........... 169
14. One Nation under Dawkins 175
15. Conclusion: A Quick Review.. 193

Copyright _ 2009

Dr. Fernandes is a "General" in the battle of defending the Christian faith. Nonetheless, even with his extensive background in apologetics, he always makes his topic reasonable and accessible to the foot soldiers who follow him. This book provides Christian soldiers with the philosophical ordnance to mount a defense of biblical Christianity.—**Dr. Ric Walston, President of Columbia Evangelical Seminary**

Atheism has made quite a comeback recently with the vitriolic attacks of the New Atheists. Are they on to something new? Have there been recent discoveries disproving the existence of God? Nothing could be further from the truth. In *The Atheist Delusion*, Phil Fernandes does a masterful job of unmasking the pretentious arguments of the New Atheists while setting forth a powerful case for Christianity. I highly recommend it.—**Sean McDowell, speaker, teacher, and co-author of *Understanding Intelligent Design***

Now here's a cloud with a very brilliant silver lining: the new militant atheists have prompted Dr. Phil Fernandes to write the most compelling, biblical and passionate Christian responses to atheism I've seen to date! This book deserves a very wide reading. It is solid, thorough, forthright and compassionate. Fernandes answers all the right questions with abundant clarity. Bravo.—**Dr. Christian Overman, author, speaker, and founder and director of *Worldview Matters***

Dr. Fernandes has a unique gift of explaining very complex and in-depth issues in a way that is efficacious for everyone. But he does this in such a way that it displays his good heart. He is both a world class scholar and a world class man. This book is evidence of that. **Matthew J. Coombe, MA (Talbot School of Theology) and vice president of the Institute of Biblical Defense**

Other Books Authored or Co-Authored by Phil Fernandes:

The God Who Sits Enthroned: Evidence for God's Existence
(Xulon Press, 2002)

No Other Gods: A Defense of Biblical Christianity
(Xulon Press, 2002)

God, Government, and the Road to Tyranny:
A Christian View of Government and Morality
(Xulon Press, 2003; co-authored with
Eric Purcell, Kurt Rinear, and Rorri Wiesinger)

Decay of a Nation: The Need for National Revival
(Triune, 1987-no longer in print)

Theism versus Atheism: The Internet Debate
(IBD Press, 1997, 2000; co-authored with Dr. Michael
Martin)

*Contend Earnestly for the Faith: A Survey of Christian
Apologetics* (Publish America, 2007)

**Phil Fernandes also contributed a chapter on
"The Absurdity of Life without God" in the following
book:**

*The Big Argument: Does God Exist? Twenty-Four Scholars
Explore How Science, Archaeology, and Philosophy Haven't
Disproved God* (Master Books, 2006)

With all my love,
to my wife Cathy,
my best friend next to Jesus.

Acknowledgments

I am forever grateful for the efforts of those who aided me in the completion of this book. Dr. Rick Walston of Columbia Evangelical Seminary has been a great help in the writing of this work. He is a great colleague and brother in Christ. The same could be said of my assistants at the Institute of Biblical Defense: Matt Coombe, Gary Tronson, Eric Stenerson, Don Davison, Robert Ostaszewski, Rorri Wiesinger, Kurt Rinear, John McCarthy, Gabe Ginorio, Matt Weeden, and Ron Kukhahn. Special thanks go to my former teachers in the field of apologetics: Dr. Gary Habermas of Liberty University and Dr. Norman Geisler, formerly of Southern Evangelical Seminary. I am also grateful to graphic artist, Bill Herod, whose cover art is second to none. Finally, my gratitude and undying love go to my precious wife Cathy. She encouraged me and believed in me when no one else did. I dedicate this book to her.

Foreword

Dr. Fernandes has long been on the front lines of the battle in Christian apologetics. I have had the privilege of knowing Phil for nearly two decades, and I am always impressed with the breadth of research and the depth of knowledge that he brings to his work, a breadth and depth that is rarely equaled.

For many years, Dr. Fernandes has been a General in the battle of defending the Christian faith. However, even with his long and rich personal and academic history in apologetics, he always makes his topic reasonable and accessible to the foot soldiers who follow him. In short, he unfolds the academically sublime in such a way as to make it food for the soul. What can be more sublime than God?

This book is not written as an emotional, knee-jerk reaction to an offending party; rather, it is a thoughtful treatise written to believers (and unbelievers as well) on the philosophical and scientific evidences for God's existence. This book is a manifest grounding for one to claim a reasonable faith in God.

A true philosopher (lover of wisdom), Dr. Fernandes does not simply call his readers to a proverbial, blind leap of empty, unsubstantiated faith, but rather he walks us through the evidences that underpin and establish true, evidential Christian faith. While some ill-informed (though well-meaning) Christians have either settled for or even promoted an anemic "faith" that is devoid of reason or evidence, no such arid and unfruitful faith is promoted here.

While faith can never be established solely on the basis of firm evidence, Dr. Fernandes understands—and helps us to understand as well—that faith is nevertheless a reasonable and rational response to the firm evidence. Atheists have historically misunderstood what true faith is. Dr. Francis S. Collins is the former director of the National Human Genome Research Institute at the National Institutes of Health. He led the successful effort to complete the Human Genome Project. He is also the author of *The Language of God: A Scientist Presents Evidence for Belief* (Free Press, 2006). In this book, Dr. Collins points up Richard Dawkins' misunderstanding of faith when he says,

> Among his many eye-popping statements [Richard Dawkins has said]: *"Faith is the great cop-out, the great excuse to evade the need to think and evaluate evidence. Faith is belief in spite of, even perhaps because of, the lack of evidence. . . . Faith, being belief that isn't based on evidence, is the principal vice of any religion."*
>
> On the other side, certain religious fundamentalists attack science as dangerous and untrustworthy, and point to a literal interpretation of sacred texts as the only reliable means of discerning scientific truth.

With neither a "faith as a cop-out" nor a "science is dangerous and untrustworthy" perspective, Dr. Fernandes brings together the reality of a genuine faith based on good science and firm evidence.

Not only is his balance refreshing, but also his timing is impeccable. As Phil says in Chapter One, "A new breed of atheists has arrived on the scene." Indeed. This new breed is more militant than ever. They are now attempting to suppress the open debate of ideas in the proverbial "public square." Sadly, too many Christians sit idly by while secularists argue for the complete removal of religion from the public square. This inertia has allowed an unprecedented, cancerous expansion of secularization in American society (as well as in Europe). The battle has become more glaring with the legal battles in Washington's State Capitol this year, 2008, over the Christmas displays. Various religions were satisfied within our pluralistic society simply to display their images without prejudice against others. That is, until the atheists put up their own "holiday plaque" which read: *"At this season of the winter solstice, may reason prevail. There are no gods, no devils, no angels, no heaven or hell. There is only our natural world. Religion is but myth and superstition that hardens hearts and enslaves minds."* Some have called it a "plaque of holiday hatred." A Nativity Scene and a Menorah peacefully coexisted side by side, but since the atheists had nothing edifying to actually promote, all that their militant display could do was go on the attack. And, if one should think that the word "attack" is hyperbole, note just this article's title from RichardDawkins.net: "Secularists' vital war on religion" by A. C. Grayling. "War." Their word, not mine. Dr. Fernandes correctly assesses the "war" and deftly warns of its consequence:

> No longer content with intellectual dialogue with Christians or others who believe in the existence of God, these new atheists use rhetoric that portrays religious believers as the main cause of the major problems we face today. Implied in their rhetoric is the idea that Christianity and traditional religions need to be silenced or removed for mankind to move forward. They seem to lack patience for 'religious people' and believe that it is time to stifle their voice.

For far too long too many Christians have stifled their own voices through their self-imposed silence, and now the new atheists are helping them to remain demur and taciturn. Not any more! In this book, Dr. Fernandes makes his voice heard, and he is calling us to stand up and be counted as well.

Atheists like Richard Dawkins and Christopher Hitchens claim that religion is evil. On this very point Joshua had this to say, "And if it seem evil unto you to serve the LORD, choose you this day whom ye will serve . . . as for me and my house, we will serve the LORD" (Joshua 24:15).

As an author, I know the frustration of not being able to say everything I want to say in a single book. Likewise, Dr. Fernandes cannot possibly deal with every nuance of all of the atheistic arguments, but he ably refutes their main arguments. Not only that, but he also provides readers (the foot soldiers) with the philosophical ordnance to mount a defense of biblical Christianity.

Ric Walston, Ph.D., President of Columbia Evangelical Seminary

Chapter One

The New, Militant Atheism

THE NEW ATHEISTS

A new breed of atheists has arrived on the scene. No longer content with intellectual dialogue with Christians or others who believe in the existence of God, these new atheists use rhetoric that portrays religious believers as the main cause of the major problems we face today. Implied in their rhetoric is the idea that Christianity and traditional religions need to be silenced or removed for mankind to move forward. They seem to lack patience for "religious people" and believe that it is time to stifle their voices.

Several of these new, militant atheists are Richard Dawkins (author of *The God Delusion*), Christopher Hitchens (author of *God is not Great-How Religion Poisons Everything*), and Sam Harris (author of *The End of Faith* and *Letter to a Christian Nation*). This book will focus on the work of Richard Dawkins and Christopher Hitchens. It will not be possible to deal with every nuance of their arguments, but we will try to refute the main points of their atheist polemic. We will also attempt to provide the reader with a general defense of biblical Christianity.

RELIGIOUS FAITH IS BLIND

Common to the teachings of the new atheists is the oversimplified idea that faith and reason do not overlap at any point. Science is the realm of pure reason, void of faith. On the other hand, religion is the realm of faith, totally void of reason. The scientific man is the man who uses his reason in an unbiased manner, whereas the religious person is the superstitious man who has thrown away his reason. These authors imply that only atheists are intellectuals—those who believe in God are superstitious persons who promote pre-scientific, antiquated beliefs that no educated person should entertain. "Religion has run out of justifications" writes Christopher Hitchens in *God is not Great*, "Thanks to the telescope and the microscope, it no longer offers an explanation of anything important."[1]

ATHEISM IS NOT A RELIGION

The new atheists blame religion for everything that goes wrong in the world. Then, they claim that atheism is not a religion. For them, the belief there is a God is a religious, superstitious belief. The rejection of belief in God is not a religious view—it is a scientific, intelligent view. In their perspective, atheism accepts the facts of the world; belief in God ignores the facts and blindly believes what no educated, twenty-first century person should believe. God, spirits, and life after death are the stuff of fairy-tales. Hitchens writes, "All religions and all churches are equally demented in their belief in divine intervention . . . and even the existence of the divine in the first place."[2] In the estimation of the new atheists, there is no more justification for a contemporary person to believe in God than there is for a person to believe in Zeus (or the Easter Bunny or the Flying Spaghetti Monster for that matter).[3]

SCIENCE HAS DISPROVEN GOD

In their view, the new atheists believe that modern science has disproved the existence of God. Since Charles Darwin published his *Origin of Species* in 1859, no educated person should entertain belief in God. According to Dawkins and Hitchens, Darwin made belief in God obsolete—everything can now be explained through natural causes alone-there is no need for believing in a supernatural cause.[4] We will see that Dawkins and Hitchens make bolder claims for Darwin's work than Darwin himself did, and that there are some scientists who reject Darwinian evolution and see in nature evidence of intelligent design.

THERE IS NO EVIDENCE FOR GOD

The new atheists believe (or at least strongly imply) that science is the only way to find truth—truth can only be found through the five senses. Since God cannot be detected through the five senses, there is no evidence He exists. Dawkins and Hitchens seem to accept the outdated belief that truth can only be found through the five senses-a belief that fails its own test for truth (since it cannot be proven to be true through the five senses). They believe that science is only allowed to search for natural causes; it is not allowed to conclude that a supernatural cause explains the natural phenomena in question.

Now, it seems obviously true that, if science is allowed to find only natural causes, then it will never find evidence for God (i.e., a supernatural cause). But, that is what the new atheists must prove, not assume. In fact, they are arguing in a circle (i.e., assuming what they are supposed to prove) when they use their own simplistic and mistaken view of science to argue against God. The founders of modern science were theists-they believed in God's existence. They saw no problem with science, at times and only when necessary, arriving at supernatural causes to explain natural effects (i.e., the beginning of the universe, the origin of life, and the origin of complex life forms).

Atheistic evolution plays the role of a religion for the new atheists. It is their ultimate truth and that which explains everything else. Dawkins and Hitchens believe that the "scientific theory" of evolution makes belief in God untenable, and therefore religion is anti-intellectual.[5]

RELIGION POISONS EVERYTHING

The new atheists believe that religion (i.e., belief in God) is the cause for all (or at least most) of the problems that have occurred throughout human history. Religion is the cause of all the wars, violence, and racism. If we want the world to be a peaceful, loving place to live, then we need to silence the voice of religion. "Religion poisons everything." These atheists stand in judgment on religion and condemn religion as being immoral.[6] Apparently Dawkins and Hitchens believe that, if atheism were universally embraced, much of the world's problems would simply go away.

EVIL AND HUMAN SUFFERING DISPROVE GOD

What makes the new atheists different from the leading atheist voices of the past is, more than anything else, their intolerant tone and their impatience with religious people. Another somewhat unique aspect of the new atheists is their total confidence in evolution as the explanation of everything that exists, though this belief was not entirely absent among some of the militant atheists of the past.

Still, they do have many points of agreement with great atheist thinkers of the past. A few examples will suffice. First, they seem to promote the idea that the amount of evil, human suffering, and death in the world is not consistent with the existence of an all-loving, all-good, all-powerful God.[7] Second, they believe that morality, whatever that may be, does not come from God; it can be accounted for merely through naturalistic explanations. Third, they reject the possibility of miracles (i.e., supernatural events). Everything that happens must have a natural cause. And, fourth, they believe there is no good historical evidence for the Jesus of the Bible.

We will show that evil, human suffering, and death are not insurmountable problems for the Christian world view. In fact, if atheism is true, it is hard to image how anything can be classified as "evil." For, if there is no ultimately good Being with His perfect will, then how can there be any perversions or violations of that perfect will. In short, evil is a perversion or corruption of the good; if the good does not exist, then what place is there for evil?

MORALITY DOESN'T COME FROM GOD

Many philosophers have argued that absolute morality must come from an absolute moral Lawgiver. However, Dawkins and Hitchens find this line of reasoning weak. They believe they can make moral judgments (i.e., they condemn Christianity and the world's major religions as being immoral) without their being any supernatural cause for morality. Assuming moral laws evolved into existence from physical matter seems to stretch credulity—but, this is what the new atheists believe.[8]

BELIEF IN MIRACLES IS SUPERSTITION

Dawkins and Hitchens still believe the outdated Enlightenment tenet of faith that miracles are impossible, or at least that they are so improbable that no intelligent person could entertain their possibility. Dawkins and Hitchens do not appear to be open to examining any evidence for a miracle claim (such as Jesus' resurrection from the dead). They a priori (before looking into the evidence) assume that miracles cannot happen. Dawkins boldly states that ". . . miracles, by definition, violate the principles of science."[9] We will show that their a priori bias against miracles is unwarranted, and that there is good historical evidence that Jesus of Nazareth rose from the dead.

THERE IS NO HISTORICAL EVIDENCE FOR THE BIBLICAL JESUS

Dawkins and Hitchens do not take Christianity seriously. They believe that, since Darwinian evolution has explained everything (in their opinion), miracle claims in different religions do not need to be investigated, or, if they are to be investigated at all, no violations of scientific principles can be allowed.[10] This is unfortunate because there is ample historical evidence that Jesus bodily rose from the dead, thus proving His claims to be God, Savior, and the Jewish Messiah are true.

TEACHING CHILDREN ABOUT GOD IS CHILD ABUSE

The new atheists believe that, since religion is the cause of most of the world's problems, teaching children about God is child abuse.[11] Since child abuse is against the law, this would seem to imply that the new atheists would like to someday see religions like Christianity outlawed. If teaching children about God is child abuse then home schooling, Christian elementary and secondary schools, and Church Sunday school programs should be abolished. At the very least, by calling it child abuse, the new atheists at least hint that religion should be abolished. Though the new atheists accuse Christians of being intolerant and claim that they—the new atheists—are extremely tolerant, it appears that the new atheists are the intolerant ones.

In the rest of this brief work, we will try to disprove the main premises of the new atheists and provide a defense for the existence of God and the biblical Jesus. The reader is encouraged to study the issues in more depth. Hence, a list of books (both pro and con) dealing with the new atheists follows this chapter.

ENDNOTES

1. Christopher Hitchens, *God Is Not Great: How Religion Poisons Everything* (New York: Hachette Book Group, 2007), 282. See also 64-65 of this same work.
2. Christopher Hitchens, "Bush's Secularist Triumph," Slate.com, November 9, 2004. Quoted in Dinesh D'Souza, *What's So Great About Christianity?* (Washington, DC: Regnery Press, Inc., 2007), 23.
3. Richard Dawkins, *The God Delusion* (Boston: Houghton Mifflin Company, 2006), 53, 55.
4. Ibid., 157-158.
5. Ibid., 158. See also Hitchens, *God is Not Great*, 282.
6. Hitchens, *God is not Great*, 173-193. Dawkins, 247-252.
7. Dawkins, 108-109.
8. Ibid., 209-233.
9. Ibid., 59.
10. Ibid., 58-61.
11. Ibid., 315-321. See also Hitchens, *God is Not Great*, 217-228.

SUGGESTED READING

The New Atheists:

Dawkins, Richard. *The God Delusion*. Boston: Houghton Mifflin Company, 2006.

Dennett, Daniel. *Breaking the Spell: Religion as a Natural Phenomenon*. New York: Viking, 2006.

Harris, Sam. *Letter to a Christian Nation*. New York: Vintage Books, 2008.

Harris, Sam. *The End of Faith*. New York: W. W. Norton and Co., 2004.

Hitchens, Christopher. *God is Not Great: How Religion Poisons Everything*. New York: Hachette Book Group, 2007.

Books Defending Belief in God:

Aikman, David. *The Delusion of Disbelief: Why the New Atheism is a Threat to Your Life, Liberty, and the Pursuit of Happiness*. Carol Stream, Illinois: Salt River, 2008.

Berlinski, David. *The Devil's Delusion: Atheism and Its Scientific Pretensions*. New York: Crown Forum, 2008.

Carroll, Vincent and David Shiflett. *Christianity on Trial: Arguments Against Anti-Religious Bigotry*. San Francisco: Encounter Books, 2002.

Dembski, William and Sean McDowell. *Understanding Intelligent Design*. Eugene: Harvest House Publishers, 2008.

D'Souza, Dinesh. *What's So Great About Christianity*. Washington, DC: Regnery Press, Inc., 2007.

Flew, Antony. *There is a God: How the World's Most Notorious Atheist Changed His Mind*. New York: Harper Collins, 2007.

Geisler, Norman L. and Frank Turek. *I Don't Have Enough Faith to Be an Atheist*. Wheaton: Crossway Books, 2004.

Habermas, Gary R. "The Plight of the New Atheism: A Critique" *Journal of the Evangelical Theological Society*. Volume 51, No. 4, December, 2008. pp.813-827.

Hahn, Scott and Benjamin Wiker. *Answering the New Atheism*. Steubenville, Ohio: Emmaus Road Publishing, 2008.

Haught, John F. *God and the New Atheism: A Critical Response to Dawkins, Harris, and Hitchens*. Louisville: Westminster John Knox Press, 2008.

Kennedy, D. James and Jerry Newcombe. *What if Jesus Had Never Been Born?* Nashville: Thomas Nelson Publishers, 1994.

Lennox, John C. *God's Undertaker: Has Science Buried God?* Oxford: Lion Hudson, 2007.

Marshall, David. *The Truth Behind the New Atheism*. Eugene, Oregon: Harvest House Publishers, 2007.

McFarland, Alex. *The 10 Most Common Objections to Christianity*. Ventura, CA: Regel Books, 2007.

McGrath, Alister and Joanna Collicut McGrath. *The Dawkins Delusion?: Atheist Fundamentalism and the Denial of the Divine*. Downers Grove, Illinois: Inter Varsity Press, 2007.

Overman, Christian. *Assumptions that Affect Our Lives*. Bellevue, WA: Ablaze Publishing Company, 2006.

Stark, Rodney. *What Americans Really Believe*. Waco: Baylor University Press, 2008.

Weikart, Richard. *From Darwin to Hitler*. New York: Palgrave Macmillan, 2004.

Zacharias, Ravi. *The End of Reason.* Grand Rapids: Zondervan, 2008.

Books on Debates between Theists and Atheists:

Fernandes, Phil and Michael Martin. *Theism vs. Atheism: The Internet Debate.* Bremerton, WA: IBD Press, 2000.

Hitchens, Christopher and Douglas Wilson. *Is Christianity Good for the World?* Moscow, ID: Canon Press, 2008.

Moreland, J. P. and Kai Nielsen. *Does God Exist? The Great Debate.* Nashville: Thomas Nelson Publishers, 1990.

Stewart, Robert B. ed. *The Future of Atheism: Alister McGrath and Daniel Dennett in Dialogue.* Minneapolis: Fortress Press, 2008.

Chapter Two

What is Religion?

WHAT IS RELIGION?

Hitchens and Dawkins proclaim that religion is something that is blindly believed, whereas atheism is evidence-based. But, is this really the case? Is belief in God a religion, but not atheism (belief that God does not exist)? Christopher Hitchens writes, "Religion has run out of justifications. Thanks to the telescope and the microscope, it no longer offers an explanation of anything important."[1]

What exactly is religion? Does someone have to believe in God to be religious? Or, is it possible for there to be non-theistic religions? If a person is religious, does that mean they cannot be scientific or rational?

IS ATHEISM A RELIGION?

Webster's Dictionary defines religion as "a specific fundamental set of beliefs and practices generally agreed upon by a number of persons or sects.[2] Atheism and agnosticism fit well in this definition. In fact, the United States Supreme Court, in the 1961 Torcaso versus Watkins Decision, ruled secular humanism (a type of atheism) to be as much a religion as theistic religions (i.e., religions that believe in a God).[3] The Supreme Court noted that even though traditional Buddhism is agnostic in reference to God's existence, no one would deny that traditional Buddhism is a religion. Even the first Humanist Manifesto of 1933, which was signed by some of the world's leading atheists and agnostics, declared secular humanism to be a religion.[4]

This seems to indicate that one does not have to believe in God to be religious. If anyone believes anything with enough passion that it impacts his or her entire life, then that person is religious. In fact, I would argue that everyone is religious. The question is not "Should a person be religious?" We already are religious. The question should be, "Which religion is true?" Even the first Humanist Manifesto stated, "Nothing human is alien to the religious."[5]

Dawkins and Hitchens seem to imply that if something cannot be placed into a test tube, we should reject its existence. But, is this really the case? We cannot place love, goodness, hope, truth, or joy into a test tube. Should we stop believing in the reality of love, goodness, hope, truth, or joy? Of course not. Some aspects of reality are non-physical, but that does not make them less real. Atheism is a reductionist philosophy that attempts to explain everything through physical causes. That does not mean that atheism is not religion. Rather, it means that atheism is a religion with very weak explanatory power.

THE ORIGIN OF RELIGION

If all people are religious, then how do we explain the origin of religion? Hitchens and Dawkins believe that religion is not based in reality. Being ardent evolutionists, they believe that somehow evolution explains the origin of religion. They are forced to speculate concerning the fact that so many people believe God exists. An example of this kind of speculation is found in the thought of Sigmund Freud, a forerunner of the new atheists.

Freud was convinced that God did not exist. But, if atheism is true, then why do so many people believe in God? Freud tried to answer this question. Freud suggested that primitive man felt extremely threatened by nature (due to storms, floods, earthquakes, diseases, and ultimately death).[6] Man had no control over nature. He was totally helpless in this regard. Primitive man was completely at the mercy of nature. There was nowhere man could turn for help. Freud theorized that primitive men therefore decided to personalize nature. In this way, man could attempt to plead with or appease nature.[7] Imagining nature to be a personal being enabled man to offer sacrifices to nature in hope that nature would be kind to him in return.

Freud's speculation did not stop there. He also promoted another theory of early human society. He assumed that originally mankind banded together in small groups. These clans consisted of a male, his several wives, and their offspring. Freud believed that, early in life, male children desired to have sex with their mothers. They therefore became extremely jealous of their father. Though they loved their father since he was their protector, they began to hate him due to their jealousy. Eventually, they banded together and murdered their father. After the murder, they ate the flesh of their father in a ritual meal. Soon, the male children were overcome with feelings of guilt. As a result, they deified the father image and began offering sacrifices to him as a god.[8]

Freud taught that God is nothing but a product of man's imagination. God did not create man. Instead, man created God. Man personalized nature due to his fear of nature. The guilt he felt for murdering his father also caused him to project the father image onto this personalized nature. In this way, reasoned Freud, the belief in the Father-God was originated by man's wishful thinking.

This highly speculative theory does not do justice to mankind's universal thirst for God. This theory appears to be "wishful thinking" on the part of Freud. Whatever the case, Freud's proposed explanation deserves a response.

A CHRISTIAN RESPONSE

Christian theologian R. C. Sproul is quick to point out that Freud's line of reasoning does not disprove God's existence.

Instead, it presupposes His nonexistence. In other words, Freud was not trying to answer the question, "Does God exist?" Rather, he was attempting to answer the question, "Since God does not exist, why do so many people believe that He does?"[9]

Therefore, this speculation by Freud should not be viewed as a disproof of God's existence. It is simply a desperate attempt to explain away strong evidence for God's existence. It is an endeavor that focuses on answering the question, "If atheism is true, why are there so few atheists?" Freud answers the question by accusing all who disagree with him of being deluded. It seems that Dawkins and Hitchens agree with this arrogant assessment-if you disagree with them on the issue of God, you are deluded. On the other hand, they are the "brights."

Sproul points out that Freud's speculation explains how men use their imaginations to invent idols (false gods) but not the God of the Bible, for the God of the Bible is far too demanding. No one would wish for the existence of a Being that requires the submission and obedience demanded by the Christian God. The gods of other religions are attractive candidates for projection, but the Holy God of the Scriptures is the type of Being from whom men run. No one would invent Him through wishful thinking.[10]

Christian philosopher J. P. Moreland states that "atheism is a result of a desire to kill the father figure (in Freudian language) because one wishes to be autonomous."[11] Man's two greatest drives are his thirst for God and his desire to be autonomous. Man has a void that can only be filled by God. Still, man wants to be his own king. The Christian chooses God over autonomy. The atheist, on the other hand, chooses autonomy.

Moreland adds that even if Freud was right, his argument would still be guilty of what philosophers call the genetic fallacy.[12] The genetic fallacy claims that a belief can be shown to be false just by showing its origin is unreasonable. But this is not the case. Even if mankind, due to fear and guilt, originated the idea of God, this does not prove that God does not exist. God might still exist even if people arrived at this conclusion through faulty reasoning.

DAWKINS' EXPLANATION FOR THE ORIGIN OF RELIGION

Dawkins knows that traditional Darwinism fails to explain the origin of religion. He also knows that the Freudian explanation cannot alone explain why so many humans are religious. Hence, Dawkins turns to the very controversial speculation about "memes" in a desperate attempt to explain the roots of religion.[13] "Memes" are defined as cultural units of information that are transmitted from one generation to another. According to Dawkins, religion is a "virus" transmitted from one brain to another. In the past, religious beliefs, though always superstitious and not based in reality, were helpful to the evolution of the human race. The belief in a reality that transcends the physical realm had many benefits, according to Dawkins, for mankind in a pre-scientific age. But, now those benefits are far outweighed by the detrimental effects of religious belief. Therefore, Dawkins believes it is time to forbid religious expression a voice in modern times. It no longer helps evolution; it now hinders it. Religion holds back human creativity. Teaching children about God is therefore harmful and should be outlawed.

In response to Dawkins' wild speculation about the origin of religion, it must be pointed out that this "explanation" presupposes that atheistic evolution is true. And, if evolution is true, we must find an explanation for the puzzling fact that about ninety percent of the world's population believes that some type of God exists. I believe it is more reasonable to be open to the possibility that ninety percent of mankind is right to believe in God, and that Dawkins and his colleagues espouse a world view that is lacking in explanatory power when it comes to such things as religion, morality, truth, self awareness, etc. When a person attempts to argue that everyone else is wrong and he is right, the burden of proof rests on him.

It should also be noted that the moral pronouncements against religion penned by Dawkins and Hitchens are inconsistent with their Darwinian belief in the chance evolution of the human race. If the human race is mere molecules in motion then, even if religion holds back or works against evolutionary progress, there is no moral standard from which to condemn religion. In fact, the idea of progress itself presupposes a moral standard, for progress implies that something is getting better. But, if there are no such things as good and evil, then there is no such thing as progress (i.e., getting better).

Dawkins' belief in "memes" as the cause of religious beliefs is unlikely at best.[14] First, there exists absolutely no scientific evidence whatsoever for memes. "Memes" is just a word atheists have invented to disguise their lack of an explanation for the origin of religion. There is no way to falsify their belief in memes. Memes have nothing to do with science—they are the product of the wild speculation of the new atheists. Memes, by definition, cannot be observed. Second, the meme is a useless hypothesis since the origin of religion can be explained adequately without invoking these "mysterious" entities. Third, the existence of memes is rejected by most scientists, even evolutionary scientists. Fourth, theists would argue that there are excellent reasons for believing in the existence of God, but there are no good reasons to believe in memes. And finally, if memes spread religious beliefs, do they also spread atheistic religious beliefs as well? If not, why not? Why do the new atheists want their atheistic religious beliefs exempted from the meme virus? It seems that memes do not explain the origin of religion. Rather, the meme is a convenient concept invented by the new atheists in an attempt to explain why so many people disagree with them and believe in God.

In the remainder of this book, we will show that belief in God (what Dawkins calls "religion") is reasonable, in fact, more reasonable than atheism. We will show that the scientific, philosophical, and historical evidence favors the Christian religion over the atheist religion. Dawkins' arguments against belief in God tend to be more of the emotional sort; solid rational argumentation is lacking in his work, as well as the work of the other new atheists.

The thesis of the new atheists assumes atheistic evolution to be true; it does not disprove or adequately explain religion. It does not build a strong case against God's existence. Once we realize that atheism is as much a religion as theistic religions then it becomes apparent that the new atheism is an intolerant religion that seeks to use science (often pseudo science) to abolish all other religions. The new atheism is a religion that seeks to force its views on others.

THE REAL PROBLEM WITH ATHEISTS

According to the Bible, the real problem with atheists is not an intellectual one. Rather it is a moral problem. It is not that there is insufficient evidence for God's existence. Instead, the atheist refuses to submit to the Creator. The Bible declares that those who act upon the truth will come to the light of Christ (John 3:16-21). On the other hand, those who suppress the truth of God's existence are without excuse, for the invisible God has revealed His existence and power through His visible creation (Romans 1:18-23).

It appears that there are two opposing drives in each person. One is a thirst for God (John 6:35); the other is the drive for human autonomy (Romans 3:10-12). If a person seeks God with all his heart, he will find Him (Jeremiah 29:13). But if he chooses to continually reject the Creator, there is no amount of evidence that will change his mind. All that the Christian apologist can do is provide evidence for the existence of the God of the Bible and refute arguments for atheism. Once a strong case for Christian Theism is made, the atheist must still choose to accept or reject the evidence. The inward persuasion of the Holy Spirit on the heart of the nonbeliever is necessary, but, in the end, the atheist must choose to follow that persuasion. The ultimate problem is not one of the intellect; it is a moral problem of the will. When all is said and done, one must choose God.

The new atheists have made their choice—apparently, no amount of evidence for God will change their minds. They claim that the existence of God is as ridiculous as the existence of a flying spaghetti monster. But, they do not write books refuting the existence of the flying spaghetti monster. They do not take debates attempting to disprove the existence of the flying spaghetti monster. And, they do not passionately speak out against the existence of the flying spaghetti monster. Their actions speak louder than their words—they attack God with all the emotions they can muster. They argue not with their intellects, but with their hearts. They ignore the rational evidence for God and instead, through their emotions and their will, they choose to reject God and devote their lives to speaking out against Him. It is as if they hate God while claiming to not even believe He exists.

ENDNOTES

1. Christopher Hitchens, *God is Not Great: How Religion Poisons Everything* (New York: Hatchett Book Group, 2007), 282.
2. *Random House Webster's College Dictionary* (New York: Random House, 1999), 1113.
3. Norman L. Geisler, *Is Man the Measure?* (Grand Rapids: Baker Book House, 1983), 164.
4. Paul Kurtz, ed. *Humanist Manifestos I and II* (Amherst: Prometheus Books, 1973), 3, 7-10.
5. Ibid., 9.
6. Sigmund Freud, *The Future of an Illusion* (Garden City, New York: Doubleday and Company, 1961), 20-27.
7. Ibid.
8. Ibid., 27, 32, 34-35.
9. R. C. Sproul, *If There's A God, Why are there Atheists?* (Wheaton: Tyndale House, 1988), 49-50.
10. Ibid., 101.
11. J. P. Moreland, *Scaling the Secular City* (Grand Rapids: Baker Book House, 1987), 229.
12. Ibid.
13. Richard Dawkins, *The God Delusion* (Boston: Houghton Mifflin Company, 2006), 191-201.
14. Robert Stewart, ed. *The Future of Atheism: Alister McGrath and Daniel Dennett in Dialogue* (Minneapolis: Fortress Press, 2008), 14-16, 30-32.

Chapter Three

Did Science Disprove God?

A Critique of Richard Dawkins' Scientific Case against God

In recent times, neo-Darwinists have gone far beyond the claims of Charles Darwin by claiming that, since evolution has explained the origin of the universe, first life, and complex life forms, there is no need for God.[1] Hence, it is claimed that belief in God is void of scientific evidence. In this paper, this view that Darwinian evolution (or some newer form of it) has disproved the existence of God will be contested. The views of Richard Dawkins will serve as an example of this Darwinian dismissal of God.

Richard Dawkins's Claim that Darwinian Evolution Disproves God

In his recent book entitled *The God Delusion*, Richard Dawkins, the former Charles Simonyi Professor of the Public Understanding of Science at Oxford University, argues that Darwinian evolution has made "the God Hypothesis untenable." He states that "God almost certainly does not exist."[2] Dawkins believes that the most plausible explanation for the "illusion of design" in living things is natural selection as defined by Darwinian evolution. He also argues that the most likely explanation for the origin of a universe like ours is the multi-verse theory.[3]

Dawkins believes that there is no need to posit the existence of the theistic God since the appearance of design in the universe, especially, in living things, has been adequately explained by Darwinian evolution. He argues that gradual and progressive evolution form the simple to the complex through natural selection has been proven. He also proposes that the multiverse theory could explain the improbable conditions necessary for life on earth, rather than resorting to belief in God. Dawkins accepts, as a more plausible explanation for the fine-tuning of the universe, the existence of innumerable parallel universes that do not overlap with each other.[4]

It appears that Dawkins' God is all-powerful chance. He is willing to invoke chance, no matter how improbable, in order to avoid admitting God created the universe. He is willing to accept wild, unbelievable natural causes rather than acknowledging a supernatural cause based on good scientific evidence. Even though he admits the universe exhibits the appearance of design, he argues that design is an illusion. After rejecting design, he then argues for the random, accidental cause of the origin of life and the existence of an innumerable amount of unverifiable, parallel universes. It seems that if science points to God, Dawkins is willing to turn to science fiction and "chance."

Dawkins dismisses "the God Hypothesis" by reasoning that if the effect (the design in the universe) is extremely improbable, then the cause (God) must be even more improbable.[5] This leads Dawkins to ask what he believes to be the question theists cannot answer: "Who designed God?"[6]

This chapter will show that Dawkins' reasoning is faulty and that Darwinian evolution has not disproved God. The unscientific assumptions of science and the limitations of science will be exposed. Finally, a scientific case against evolution and for creation will be made. First, Dawkins's faulty reasoning will be addressed.

Dawkins's Faulty Reasoning

Dawkins attacks the teleological argument for God (i.e., the argument for God's existence from design in the universe) by reasoning that if the effect (a universe compatible for human life) is highly improbable, then the cause (God) must be even more improbable.[7] But, this is simply mistaken, for the theist does not argue that a universe fine-tuned for life is improbable in itself. To the contrary, a universe fine-tuned for life is only improbable if it came into being totally by chance. The theist argues that the design found in the universe to support human life could not have come about through non-intelligent causes—the universe must have been designed by an intelligent Being. If God exists then the existence of a universe designed for human life is not improbable—for an intelligent Being planned the universe to be suited for human life.

An illustration offered by Christian philosopher Norman Geisler makes this point well.[8] Geisler argues that the formation of the faces on Mount Rushmore would be highly improbable, if not impossible, through natural means alone. However, if they were produced by intelligent design, then their appearance would not be improbable. This is exactly the case with the design found in the universe—it is only improbable if no intelligent Designer exists. If the intelligent Designer exists, then the design in the universe is not improbable since the Designer planned it that way.

Dawkins is also mistaken when he asks the question, "Who designed God?" His question misses the point. If finite, temporal, changing beings exist, then there must exist an infinite, eternal, unchanging Being to ground their existence.[9] One cannot have an infinite regress of designers; eventually, one will arrive at the eternal Designer. The theist is not *begging* the question by arguing for an eternal, infinite Designer—he is *answering* the question as to how finite design exists in the universe. Complex design needs an intelligent Designer; but, if the intelligent Designer is eternal, then the Designer does not itself need a Designer—He always existed.

The Assumptions and Limitations of Science

Dawkins implies throughout his work that science is the only valid way for man to find truth.[10] Again, Dawkins is simply mistaken. In order for scientific investigation to begin, the scientists must make several assumptions—assumptions that cannot be proven through science (i.e., through the five senses). The scientist must assume that a real world exists outside his mind, his senses are reliable and not deceiving him, and truth and honesty are real.[11] A scientist cannot prove through experimentation that the real world exists outside his mind, for in his attempt to prove this, he assumes its existence as he uses his five senses to study this world. To do science, a scientist must trust the data discovered through his five senses. Science does not prove the basic reliability of the five senses—it presupposes it. Likewise, the scientist assumes real truths exist that can be found through science, and that the results of his experimentation should be honestly reported. Yet, truth cannot be placed in a test tube; it cannot be weighed or examined. Science presupposes truth is real, but has no way of proving it is real. And honesty is a moral virtue that also cannot be examined through the five senses. In short, the existence of a real world outside the human mind, the basic reliability of sense perception, the existence of truth, and the reality of moral virtues like honesty cannot be proven through science. These are not scientific issues at all—they are philosophical assumptions that the scientist must make to justify the scientific endeavor.[12]

Another way of showing that science is not the only avenue through which truth can be found is by showing the self-refuting nature of such a claim. The statement "Truth can only be found through the five senses" is a self-refuting statement. It cannot be true, for the statement itself cannot be proven to be true by the five senses. Therefore, there are other ways of finding truth than through the five senses (i.e., science).[13]

This shows us that science is limited in its scope-there are truths that exist that cannot be found through the five senses alone. This would include moral laws, the concept of truth, virtues like love, and the concept of meaning in life.[14] Despite the fact that Dawkins wants to proclaim science as the only arbiter of truth and knowledge, there are some truths and issues that are simply outside the field of science. These truths are in the domains of philosophy and religion. To argue that science alone can find truth is an extremely dogmatic stance that cannot be justified by the evidence.

Dawkins is a naturalist—he believes that all explanations must be physical explanations. This makes him a proponent of what has been labeled "scientism."[15] Scientism goes beyond the limited scope of science and demands that only natural or physical explanations can be accepted—no non-physical or supernatural explanations are allowed—they are ruled out a priori (i.e., before any investigation of the evidence). While true science examines physical effects and goes wherever the evidence leads (whether it be a natural or supernatural cause), scientism dismisses any possibility of a supernatural or non-physical cause at the outset. Hence, scientism is not good science; it is a dogmatic bias against possible supernatural or non-natural causes. Scientism is a prejudiced look at the evidence—it is not an objective, unbiased attempt to find truth.[16]

Therefore, the failure of naturalism/scientism to justify itself must be noted. Ronald Nash shows the futility of naturalism's attempt to justify itself by referring to the work of C. S. Lewis and Richard Taylor.[17] Nash argues that all our knowledge depends upon the validity of human reason; for if our reasoning ability is not valid, then we have no reason to trust the conclusions drawn by our reason. No scientific discoveries or claims to knowledge can be trusted if our reason does not work. If naturalism is true, then there is no basis for our faith in human reason.[18]

Nash discusses an illustration given by Richard Taylor. If a lady is on a train entering Wales and she sees white stones on a hillside spelling out "Welcome to Wales," she is free to believe, however unlikely it may be, that the white stones randomly spelled out that message and that no intelligence placed the stones in that specific order to communicate the message that travelers are now entering Wales. But, if she believes that the order of the white stones was a product of random causes, then she has no basis for trusting what the white stones tell her. She has no basis for believing the message is true and that she is now entering Whales. The same dilemma occurs for the naturalist. The naturalist, like Dawkins, is free to believe that human reasoning ability got here by chance and is not a product of rational causes. But, then the naturalist has no reason to trust what his reason tells him. Naturalists believe our reason got here by chance; therefore, they have no reason to believe that their reason works. Hence, naturalists have no reason to believe that naturalism is true. In short, if naturalism is true then there is no way to know that it is true.[19] Dawkins' naturalism is accepted by blind faith. Apparently he is not the unbiased, rational "Bright" that he claims to be.[20] While slamming religious people for faith, even Dawkins has his own faith. But, his faith is blind and not supported by the evidence.

Dawkins' Mistaken View of Faith and Reason

Dawkins' blind naturalism stems from his mistaken view of faith and reason. He wrongly assumes that, by definition, faith and reason are mutually exclusive. He believes that, by definition, religious faith is blind and science alone is rational.[21] This is clearly a straw man argument. Many religious people, like this author, consider their faith to be based firmly on strong evidence. Merely because Dawkins assumes all religious faith is non-rational or irrational does not mean that this is the case.

Even scientists must exercise faith. Scientists, as mentioned above, place faith in the reliability of the five senses and the existence of a real physical world existing independently of their minds. These cannot be proven through the five senses alone. In a debate with Oxford scholar John Lennox, Dawkins admitted that he has good reasons for the faith he has in his wife, thus contradicting his own view.[22] Hence, faith and reason are not mutually exclusive. When someone drives his car over a cement bridge suspended hundreds of feet above the ground, he is displaying great faith in man's technology to build adequate bridges. This is not blind faith, but a faith built upon evidence. Many Christians believe their faith is not blind and that it is based upon evidence.

In fact, contrary to what Dawkins believes, a case can made that all people are religious. If when the Christian says "God exists," he is uttering a religious statement, then when the atheist declares "God does not exist," he is also uttering a religious statement. The subject does not change simply be the negating of an affirmation. If the belief that there is a God is a religious belief, then the belief there is no God is also a religious believe. As noted earlier, this point can be confirmed in several ways.

First, Webster's Dictionary provides as one of the definitions of religion: "a specific fundamental set of beliefs and practices generally agreed upon by a number of persons or sects."[23] Atheists and agnostics share common fundamental beliefs and practices, thus placing them clearly in the "religious" camp.

Second, the 1961 Torcaso versus Watkins Supreme Court Decision declared secular humanism to be as much a religion as theistic religions.[24] The court noted that traditional Buddhism is agnostic concerning the existence of God, yet no one denies that traditional Buddhism is a religion. Hence, one does not have to believe in God to be religious.

Third, the first Humanist Manifesto, written in 1933 and signed by some of the world's leading atheists and agnostics, declares secular humanism to be a religion.[25] Secular humanism is a belief system that is based on the belief there is no God and that the universe got here through naturalistic causes alone.

Hence, all people are religious; all people hold deeply cherished beliefs and build their lives upon the foundation of those beliefs. Even the apathetic person builds his life upon his apathy. Even the skeptic is dogmatic about his skepticism. "Nothing human is alien to the religious."[26] This is as true for the atheist as it is for the Christian or other theists. Therefore, Dawkins' dogmatic belief that religious people have irrational faith whereas atheists accept only what can be rationally proven is simply not true. Dawkins is as religious as Christians or theists. The question is not "Should I be religious?" Everyone, including Dawkins, already is. Instead, the question should be "Is my religion based on the evidence or refuted by the evidence?" If Dawkins is not religious, then why does he write with so much passion and religious fervor?

The History of the Contemporary Creation-Evolution Debate

Today, many people believe that evolution is a biological fact. However, this is not the case. Science, by definition, deals with probabilities, not certainties. My case for creation will draw heavily upon the information found in the book *Origin Science* by Norman L. Geisler and J. Kirby Anderson.[27]

The creation model is the view that God created the universe without using evolution. The creation model dominated modern science before 1860.[28] Modern science was started by men who believed in the existence of the God of the Bible. Galileo, Isaac Newton, Francis Bacon, Johannes Kepler, and Blaise Pascal are just a few who fit into this category.[29] Their belief in God's existence formed the foundation for modern science. They believed that a reasonable God created the universe in a reasonable way, so that through reason man could find out about the universe in which he lives.[30] In other words, the universe makes sense only because God designed it to make sense. Today, however, atheistic evolutionists, like Richard Dawkins, have rejected this base for modern science.[31] They have rejected the existence of a reasonable God. But the question that they must face is this: "Without a reasonable God, can a person really expect the universe to make sense?" Therefore, one should not forget the Christian roots of modern science.

The evolution model is the view that life spontaneously evolved from non-life without intelligent intervention.[32] The evolution model dominated modern science after 1860.[33] Charles Darwin published his book *The Origin of Species* around that time (i.e., 1859).[34] Darwin proposed a naturalistic explanation for the origin of the universe, first life, and new life forms.[35] He taught that nature can be explained without appealing to a supernatural origin. Darwin's proposal quickly became the predominant "scientific" view.

The Distinction between Origin Science and Operation Science

Though Dawkins may treat it as such, we need to understand that evolution is not a scientific fact. The scientific method consists of six steps: 1) observation, 2) proposal of a question or problem, 3) hypothesis (an educated guess), 4) experimentation, 5) theory (a hypothesis with a high degree of probability), and 6) natural law (a theory thought to be valid on a universal scale).[36] Evolution is not a scientific law or theory, let alone a scientific fact. The supposed evolutionary changes from one species to another cannot be observed.[37] They supposedly occurred in the past. Therefore, since observation is the initial step in the scientific method, evolution cannot be proven through the scientific method.

Geisler and Anderson point out that the creation view is in the same category as evolution. Creation, scientifically speaking, is not a fact, law, or theory. Like evolution, the supposed creation is a singular event in the past. It cannot be observed. Therefore, both creation and evolution are only *scientific models*; they represent different ways to interpret the same evidence.[38]

This does not mean that creation and evolution cannot claim to be scientific. Contrary to popular belief, the scientific method is not the only way to search for truth in the field of science. Geisler and Anderson point to forensic science as an example. Forensic science (crime scene investigation) does not use the scientific method, for the crime can no longer be observed. Still, forensic science is a legitimate science.[39] Science can be separated into two main divisions: operation science and origin science. Operation science deals with the repeatable; it is science of the observable present. It uses the scientific method. Forensic science, creation, and evolution do not fall into this category.[40] Origin science, on the other hand, deals with the non-repeatable; it deals with the singular events of the past. Origin science does not utilize the scientific method since singular events of the past can no longer be observed.[41] Geisler and Anderson inform us that forensic science, creation science, and evolutionary science fall into this category (i.e., origin science).

Since the non-repeatable events of the past cannot be observed, origin science does not make use of the scientific method. Instead, origin science uses the principles of analogy (also called uniformity) and causality to determine whether or not a model is plausible.[42] The principle of analogy states that when a scientist observes a cause bringing about a certain effect in the present, he should posit the same kind of cause for a similar effect in the past.[43] In other words, similar effects usually have similar causes. The principle of causality states that every event must have an adequate cause.[44] A scientist should use these two principles to determine the plausibility (or lack of plausibility) of a particular model.

Since the creation model and the evolution model fall under the heading of origin science, the principles of analogy and uniformity must be applied to them to determine which model is more plausible. It must be understood that the creation model and the evolution model both deal with the same evidence. An example of this is common anatomy. Common anatomy deals with the similarities in the body parts of different species. Examples of common anatomy are the similarities that exist concerning the arm of a man, the arm of an ape, the wing of a bird, and the fin of a shark. Both creationists and evolutionists agree to the common anatomy between different species of animal life. However, the two models interpret the evidence differently. The evolution model teaches that common anatomy proves common ancestry.[45] Common ancestry is the view that all species are related since one species has evolved into another. The creation model teaches that the same data (common anatomy) proves the existence of a common Designer. Animals often share common anatomy due to their being created and designed by the same God.[46]

Which model is more plausible? In order to answer this question, the principles of analogy and causality must be applied to the origin of the universe, the origin of first life, and the origin of new life forms. Both the creation model and the evolution model must be tested in these three areas to ascertain which model is more plausible. It is important to note that Geisler and Anderson show us that, as we study nature, we are not to assume that the cause will automatically be a natural cause. We must go wherever the evidence will lead. This is in direct opposition to the scientific naturalism (i.e., scientism) of Richard Dawkins. He rules out any possibility of a supernatural cause at the outset. But, this is not good science—good science will go wherever the evidence leads.

The Origin of the Universe

Did the universe have a beginning, or did it always exist? This is a very important question, for if the universe had a beginning, it would need a cause. It could not have evolved into existence from nothing. If the universe is eternal then it may not need a cause. Fortunately, science is not silent on this question.

Geisler and Anderson identify several evidences that the universe had a beginning. These evidences for the beginning of the universe are also confirmed by Christian philosopher William Lane Craig. The second law of thermodynamics is called energy deterioration. This law says that the amount of usable energy in any closed system like the universe is running down.[47] Eventually, all the energy in the universe will be used up. This means that the universe is winding down. If it is winding down, it had to have been "wound up." If the universe is going to have an end, it had to have a beginning. There had to be a time when all the energy in the universe was usable; this marks the beginning of the universe.

The expansion of the universe and the big bang model also confirm the beginning of the universe.[48] In 1929, astronomer Edwin Hubble discovered that the universe is expanding at the same rate in all directions.[49] As time moves forward the universe is growing apart. This means that if one went back in time the universe would get denser. If one goes back in time far enough, the entire universe would be contained in what scientists have called "a point of infinite density."[50] But, a point can only be finitely dense, for if a physical point was infinitely dense it would have to be non-existent. Therefore, the universe came into existence from nothing a finite time ago.

There have been two main attempts to refute the proposition that the universe had a beginning. The first is the steady-state model. This view holds that the universe had no beginning. Instead, it always existed in the same state. However, because of the mounting evidence for the big bang model, this view has been abandoned by most of its adherents.[51]

The second attempt to evade the beginning of the universe is called the oscillating model. This model teaches that, at some point during the universe's expansion, gravity will halt the expansion and pull everything back together again. From that point there will be another big bang. This process will be repeated over and over again throughout all eternity. However, Craig states that the oscillating model fails for three reasons. First, there is no known principle of physics that would reverse the expansion of the universe into another big bang. Second, current scientific research has shown that the universe is not dense enough for gravity to pull it back together again. Third, even if one could prove that several big bangs have occurred, the second law of thermodynamics would still require that there was a first big bang.[52]

Therefore, science has shown that the universe had a beginning, but, since from nothing, nothing comes, something must have caused the universe to come into existence. Everything that has a beginning needs a cause. Since the universe needs a cause, the creation model is more plausible than the evolution model. If the universe were eternal, then the evolution model could claim some type of plausibility. But, for the above reasons, this is not the case. The universe is not eternal; it had a beginning. Something separate from the universe had to cause it to come into existence. Hence, the present state of atheism has been reduced to the belief that the universe came into existence by nothing and from nothing. But, since nothing is nothing, it can do nothing. (Only actual existing things can have the power to do things.) If nothing can do nothing, it can cause nothing. If the universe had an absolute beginning, something else must have caused it to exist. If all of nature needs a cause, then, by definition, the cause must be a supernatural cause. Hence, in regards to the beginning of the universe, the creation model is more plausible than the evolution model.

The Origin of First Life

Evolution teaches spontaneous generation—that life came from non-life without intelligent intervention.[53] However, spontaneous generation violates the law of biogenesis and the cell theory. The law of biogenesis states that "all living things arise only from other living things."[54] The cell theory defines the cell as the most basic unit of life, and declares that "new cells arise only from pre-existing cells."[55] Both the law of biogenesis and the cell theory are accepted by evolutionists; the evolutionists merely assume that first life is the exception to these principles. But, a model that violates scientific theories and laws should be abandoned. This is especially true when there is a rival model that does not violate scientific theories and laws.

The creation model posits the existence of an intelligent Being in order to bridge the gap from non-life to life. The creation model recognizes that the specified complexity (highly complex information) found in a single-celled animal could not be produced by chance. Even Richard Dawkins himself believes that a single-celled animal contains enough genetic information to fill one-thousand complete sets of the Encyclopedia Britannica.[56] Just as an explosion in a print shop cannot randomly produce even one volume of an encyclopedia (not to mention one-thousand complete sets), there is no way that a single-celled animal could have been produced by mere chance. Intelligent intervention was needed.[57]

Natural laws by themselves do not produce specified complexity. Geisler illustrates this point by stating that though natural laws can explain the Grand Canyon, they cannot explain the faces on Mount Rushmore.[58] The faces on Mount Rushmore reveal evidence of intelligent design.

Evolutionists often offer the Miller and Urey experiments as evidence that life has been produced from non-life in the laboratory. In response, several things should be noted. First, Chandra Wickramasinghe, one of Britain's most eminent scientists, calls these experiments "cheating." Miller and Urey start with amino acids, break them down, and then recover them. They do not produce something that wasn't there to begin with.[59] Second, Geisler states that the Miller and Urey experiments do not produce life. They only produce amino acids, which are the building blocks of life. Amino acids are to life what a single sentence is to one-thousand complete sets of encyclopedia.[60] Third, Geisler points out that even if these experiments did produce life from non-life in the laboratory (which they don't), it would support the creation model, not the evolution model. The reason for this is clear. The experiments would merely prove that to get life from non-life intelligent intervention (i.e., the scientists) is needed. The experiments would not prove that life spontaneously arose from non-life.[61]

Therefore, the creation model is more plausible than the evolution model when explaining the origin of first life. Intelligent intervention is necessary to produce life from non-life. It could not have happened by accident.

The Origin of New Life Forms

Many people believe that the fossil record proves evolution, but, this is not the case. In the fossil record, new life forms appear suddenly and fully developed.[62] There is no evidence of transitional forms (missing links). There are no fins or wings becoming arms. There are no intermediate forms. The gaps between major groups in the fossil record are evidence against evolution, not for evolution.

Evolution teaches that single-celled animals eventually evolved into human beings. Of course, evolutionists claim this took long periods of time to be accomplished. A single-celled animal contains enough information to fill one-thousand complete sets of encyclopedia,[63] but the human brain contains enough information to fill twenty million volumes of encyclopedia.[64] Natural law, no matter how much time is involved, can never produce twenty million volumes of encyclopedia from one-thousand complete sets of encyclopedia. Intelligent intervention is needed to produce more complex information.[65]

Evolutionists often point to mutations as the process by which evolution takes place.[66] However, mutations do not add more complex information to the genetic code. Instead, they merely garble the already existing genetic code.[67] For evolution to

35

take place, new genetic information is needed. For example, single-celled animals would need new genes for the development of teeth, yet mutations produce no new genetic information.[68]

Simple life forms do not go to complex life forms through natural law alone.[69] Time plus chance plus natural laws can never produce more complex information.[70] Something must impart more information. Therefore, the creation model is more plausible than the evolution model concerning the origin of new life forms.

The superiority of the creation model is clearly seen through what scientists refer to as the anthropic principle. Simply put, this principle teaches that, when the universe is examined closely, it appears as if it has been fine-tuned to support human life on the planet earth. Astrophysicist Hugh Ross has listed twenty-five narrowly defined parameters that the universe had to have in order for life to be possible.[71] Ross has also pointed out thirty-two narrowly defined parameters for life to be possible concerning the earth, its moon, its sun, and its galaxy.[72] For instance, if the distance between the earth and the sun was to differ by just two percent in either direction, no life on earth would be possible.[73] These parameters for life on earth clearly show evidence that the universe was designed for life. The creation model of intelligent design is more plausible than the evolutionary model of random chance.

In a desperate attempt to explain away the anthropic principle, Dawkins places his faith in the highly speculative multiverse view[74] This view suggests the existence of an infinite number of parallel universes that do not overlap. It is argued that if there were an infinite number of universes that were randomly produced, then one of these universes would have to have all the supposed order and complexity and design that we find in our universe today. Hence, it should be no surprise that we find the illusion of order, complexity, and design in the universe in which we live.

There are numerous problems with this highly speculative theory. First, this is not a scientific view at all, for, since the universes do not overlap, there is no scientific way to verify their existence. The parallel universes can never be observed, nor can any evidence of their existence be found in this universe. Hence, the multiverse view is metaphysical, religious, or philosophical; but, it is not scientific-it is not the result of examining the universe through the five senses.[75] Second, the burden of proof lies clearly with those who argue for the existence of more universes than the only one we experience. Third, the tremendous amount of information needed for these multiple universes still necessitates the existence of an intelligent Designer. And, fourth, the multiverse theory is as Hugh Ross wrote "a flagrant abuse of probability theory." Ross stated that "it assumes the benefits of a infinite sample size without any evidence that the sample size exceeds one."[76] Therefore, the belief in the existence of an intelligent Being who designed the universe is more plausible than the non-verifiable belief in the existence of infinite parallel universes.

Hence, the scientific case for creation is very strong. Though it is true that creationists have never seen the invisible Creator, evolutionists also have never seen the supposed evolutionary changes of the past. The principles of analogy and causality support creationism as a superior model to evolution. Blind chance and natural laws are inadequate causes for the origin of the universe, first life, and new life forms. An intelligent Cause is needed in each case. The cause of the beginning of nature cannot be nature itself. No being can pre-exist its own existence in order to cause its own existence. Therefore, nature needs a supernatural Cause. This supernatural Cause must be an intelligent Being to bring life from non-life and complex life forms from simple life forms. Hence, as Geisler and Anderson have shown, the creation model is more plausible than the evolution model.

The Scientific Case against Evolution

At this point, the scientific case against evolution will be discussed. There are major problems with the evolution model that render it obsolete as an explanation of the available scientific data. We will comment briefly on these problem areas. Thermo-dynamics deals with the relationship between heat, energy, and work.[77] The first and second laws of thermodynamics pose serious problems for evolution. The first law of thermodynamics is called energy conservation. It states that the amount of energy in the universe remains constant; no energy is now being created or destroyed.[78] This means that if the universe had a beginning, whatever process or act that brought the universe into existence is no longer in operation today. In other words, the "creation process" is no longer operating today. Therefore, either the universe is eternal or the universe was created in the past; no continuing creative process is occurring.

The second law of thermodynamics is called entropy. Though the amount of energy in the universe remains constant, it changes form. The second law states that when energy changes form it becomes less usable.[79] Therefore, the amount of usable energy in the universe is running out. This means that the day will come when all the energy in the universe will have been used up. This will be the death of the universe. There must have been a time when all the energy of the universe was usable; this would be the beginning of the universe. In other words, since the universe is going to have an end, it is not eternal. If it is not eternal, then it must have had a beginning. The big bang model and the expansion of the universe also confirm the beginning of the universe.[80]

The evolutionist faces a dilemma. The first and second laws of thermodynamics together implicitly declare that the universe had a beginning. The evolutionists cannot deny these laws, for they are considered to be the most firmly established laws of modern science.[81] But, evolution runs counter to these two laws. When a scientific model contradicts a scientific law, the model should be abandoned. Since the first and second laws of thermodynamics

38

teach that the universe had a beginning, then something outside the universe must have caused the universe to come into existence. For, from nothing, nothing comes. Therefore, the universe could not have come into existence out of nothing.

The fossil record is assumed to prove evolution, but, this is not the case. The fossil record shows no evidence of transitional forms (missing links). New life forms appear suddenly and fully developed.[82] There are no animals with half-fins or half-wings in the fossil record. If there were transitional forms, why have none been found? This is a serious problem for evolutionists. Harvard paleontologists Stephen Jay Gould and Louis Agassiz have admitted this lack of evidence for evolution in the fossil record.[83] Aggassiz, a nineteenth-century creationist, stated:

Species appear suddenly and disappear suddenly in the progressive strata. . . . the supposed intermediate forms between the species of different geological periods are imaginary beings, called up merely in support of a fanciful theory.[84]

Gould, a twentieth century evolutionist, stated: "In any local area, a species does not arise gradually by the steady transformation of its ancestors; it appears all at once and 'fully formed.'"[85] Hence, a devastating problem for the evolution model is the lack of transitional forms.

No one possesses an undisputed missing link. All the supposed missing links between apes and men have been dismissed. Neanderthal Man and Cro-Magnon Man both have the features of modern man.[86] Colorado Man turned out to be a member of the horse family.[87] Java Man (also known as Pithecanthropus) was shown to be the remains of a large gibbon.[88] Heidelberg Man consisted of only a lower jaw.[89] Obviously, a lower jaw is insufficient evidence for a missing link. One can only speculate as to the makeup of the rest of the skull and skeleton. The Piltdown Man was revealed to be a clever hoax.[90] The Peking

Man is now thought to be a large monkey or baboon.[91] The Southern Ape (also called Australopithecus), Dryopithecus, and Ramapithecus were extinct apes.[92] The East African Man (Zinjanthropus) was shown to be an ape.[93] Finally, the Nebraska Man, which consisted of only one tooth, was proven to be the tooth of an extinct pig.[94] This is rather interesting since this tooth had been presented as evidence in the 1925 "monkey trial" as "evidence" for the evolutionary model.[95] When the tooth of an extinct pig is mistaken for the tooth of the missing link between apes and men, it shows how subjective modern science has become. Though high school and college textbooks show drawings of the missing links from apes to men, the fact is that this art merely depicts the vivid imagination of scientists. No undisputed missing link between apes and men has been discovered.

Archaeopteryx was once thought to be a transitional form between reptiles and birds.[96] It had features resembling that of a reptile (teeth, lizard-like tail, and claws). But, archaeopteryx also had wings and feathers similar to a bird. Still, the archaeopteryx was fully developed. It did not have half-wings or the like. Archaeopteryx has now been classified as a bird. This is due to the fact that every characteristic of archaeopteryx can be found in some genuine bird, though some of its features are not found in reptiles.[97] It should also be noted that the supposed evolution of reptiles into birds is highly improbable. The lungs of a reptile have millions of tiny air sacs, while the lungs of birds have tubes. In order for a transitional form to exist between a reptile and a bird it would have to breathe without having fully-developed lungs,[98] and this is an impossibility. Evolutionists believe that invertebrates (animals without backbones) have evolved into vertebrates (animals with backbones). However, no transitional form between the two has ever been found.[99]

This lack of transitional forms is very problematic for the evolution model. It has been nearly 150 years since Darwin wrote *The Origin of Species*. Still, no missing links have been found. Due to this absence of evidence for evolution, modern evolutionists like Stephen Jay Gould have proposed a new model called "Punctuated Equilibrium."[100] Whereas evolution means "gradual change,"

Punctuated Equilibrium teaches that the changes occurred so suddenly that transitional forms did not survive long enough to be fossilized. It appears that Punctuated Equilibrium is an attempt to explain away the absence of evidence for evolution—but it fails as well.

Since there is no evidence of missing links in the fossil record, evolution should be rejected. The lack of transitional forms in the fossil record is evidence against evolution and in favor of the creation model, which teaches that there are no missing links.[101]

Evolutionists need a mechanism that explains how evolution has supposedly occurred. Many evolutionists believe that mutation is this mechanism.[102] However, mutations merely scramble the already existing genetic code. No new genetic information is added.[103] Yet, for evolution to have occurred, a mechanism is needed through which new genes are produced. Therefore, mutations fail to explain evolution. Evolutionists claim that they believe the present interprets the past. However, there is no mechanism in the present that spontaneously produces new genetic information. Until such a mechanism is found, evolution can only be accepted by "blind faith."

Hence, evolution is not a proven fact. It is assumed to be true by many scientists, but they have offered no convincing proofs. There is no evidence for the evolution model. This can be seen in the many unproven assumptions held by evolutionists.

First, there is no evidence for spontaneous generation. The belief that life evolved from non-life contradicts both the cell theory and the law of biogenesis. The Miller-Urey experiments have failed to produce life in the lab (if they were successful, it would be evidence for the creation model not the evolution model).

Second, there is no evidence for the nineteenth century evolutionary assumption that the universe is eternal. Evolutionists who want to retain this antiquated belief must accept this by faith. Most evolutionists today assume that the universe burst into existence from nothing, but this assumption goes against all available scientific evidence (we do not see this occurring today) as well as logic itself. Nonbeing cannot cause being; from nothing, nothing comes. Nothing is nothing; therefore, nothing can do nothing; hence, nothing can cause nothing. It is not possible for the universe to have been brought into existence by absolute nothing.

Third, there is no evidence that intelligence could come from non-intelligence. Intelligence shows evidence of design; it could not have been produced by chance. And, if human intelligence was produced by chance, then how can we trust what it tells us?

Fourth, no evidence has been found proving that multi-celled animals came from single-celled animals. (Even the human embryo does not evolve into a human; it has its full human genetic code at conception.)[104]

Fifth, there is no evidence for the evolution of animals with backbones from animals without backbones.[105] Though there should be multitudes of transitional forms between the two groups, none have been found.

Sixth, there is no evidence for the common ancestry of fish, reptiles, birds, and mammals.[106] Common anatomy could point to a common Designer; it does not necessarily point to common ancestry.

All the major gaps that evolution must cross are assumed to have occurred; they have not been proven to have occurred. Therefore, evolution itself is an unproven assumption. Those, like Richard Dawkins, who dogmatically proclaim evolution as truth spend more time explaining away the scientific evidence against their view than they do providing evidence for their view. Any scientific model that lacks plausibility should be abandoned. Such is the case with evolution.

Concluding Remarks

In his recent work entitled *The God Delusion*, Richard Dawkins argues that human reason proves that evolution is true and that "the God hypothesis" is outdated and should be rejected. This paper has exposed Richard Dawkins' faulty reasoning, showed that science is not the only road to truth, and critiqued Dawkins' weak view of faith and reason. The scientific case for creation proposed by Norman Geisler and J. Kirby Anderson was discussed, as well as a scientific case against evolution. This chapter has shown that the major tenets of evolution are assumed, not proven, by evolutionists. Hence, evolution is itself an assumption, not a confirmed scientific model.

In conclusion, Dawkins' thesis that the God hypothesis is untenable is itself untenable. This chapter has shown that evolution needs God, but God does not need evolution. If evolution is true, then God is needed to bring the universe into existence from nothing, to bring life from non-life, and complex life forms from simple life forms. In each case, a miraculous superseding of natural laws is needed. However, if God exists, He does not need evolution. He could have either started the long evolutionary process or He could have created the universe in six literal days. God could have used evolution, but if He did, He covered His tracks. He left no evidence. Since God is not the author of deception, it is reasonable to conclude that evolution is a myth and that evolution has not disproven God.

ENDNOTES

1. Contrary to popular belief, Charles Darwin did not believe his "scientific" views disproved the existence of God. He began his research as a theist who questioned the absolute authority of the Bible concerning scientific matters. He began his studies as a creationist, but became an evolutionist between 1835 and 1837. Darwin gradually became a deist and this was his view by the time he wrote *The Origin of Species* in 1859. Darwin did not consider himself an agnostic until about 1879. See Norman L. Geisler, *History of Modern and Contemporary Philosophy-AP506 Lecture Notes* (Charlotte: Southern Evangelical Seminary, 2005), 46-63. Hence, Darwin did not believe his views had disproven the existence of God. The claims of neo-Darwinians like the late Carl Sagan and Richard Dawkins are much bolder. Sagan wrote, "The Cosmos is all that is or ever was or ever will be" in his *Cosmos* (London: Futura Publications, 1983), 20.
2. Richard Dawkins, *The God Delusion* (Boston: Houghton Mifflin Company, 2006), 158.
3. Ibid., 145-147, 158.
4. Ibid.
5. Ibid., 143, 151.
6. Ibid., 113-114, 158.
7. Ibid., 147, 158.
8. Norman L. Geisler and J. Kirby Anderson, *Origin Science: A Proposal for the Creation-Evolution Controversy* (Grand Rapids: Baker Book House, 1987), 159-164.
9. Norman L. Geisler, *Christian Apologetics* (Grand Rapids: Baker Book House, 1976), 242-247.
10. Dawkins, *The God Delusion*, 14, 58-66. See also John F. Haught's description of scientific naturalism, a view held by Dawkins and rejected by Haught, in *God and the New Atheism* (Louisville: Westminster John Knox Press, 2008), 41.

11. John C. Lennox, *God's Undertaker: Has Science Buried God?* (Oxford: Lion Books, 2007), 31-45. See also J. P. Moreland, *Christianity and the Nature of Science* (Grand Rapids: Baker Book House, 1989), 103-138.
12. Ibid.
13. Norman L. Geisler and Paul D. Feinberg, *Introduction to Philosophy: A Christian Perspective* (Grand Rapids: Baker Book House, 1980), 50-51.
14. Lennox, 38-43.
15. Haught, 17. See also Dinesh D'Souza, *What's So Great About Christianity* (Washington, DC: Regnery Publishing, 2007), 160-164.
16. Ibid.
17. Ronald Nash. 1997. "Miracles and Conceptual Systems" in *In Defense of Miracles*, eds. Douglas R. Geivett and Gary R. Habermas, 115-131. Downers Grove: InterVarsity Press.
18. Ibid., 127-130.
19. Ibid., 130-131.
20. Dawkins, *The God Delusion*, 338.
21. Lennox, 15-16.
22. This occurred in a 2007 debate between John Lennox and Richard Dawkins.
23. *Random House Webster's College Dictionary* (New York: Random House, 1999), 1113.
24. Norman L. Geisler, *Is Man the Measure?* (Grand Rapids: Baker Book House, 1983), 164.
25. Paul Kurtz, ed. *Humanist Manifestos I and II* (Amherst: Prometheus Books, 1973), 3, 7-10.
26. Ibid., 9.
27. Geisler and Anderson.
28. Ibid., 37-52.
29. Ibid.
30. Ibid., 37-40, 51.
31. Ibid., 52.
32. Ibid., 82-86.
33. Ibid.
34. Ibid.

35. Ibid.
36. Tom M. Graham, *Biology, the Essential Principles* (Philadelphia: Saunders College Publishing, 1982), 6.
37. Geisler and Anderson, 15-18.
38. Ibid., 18, 25.
39. Ibid., 25, 116.
40. Ibid., 106.
41. Ibid., 105-106.
42. Ibid., 130-132.
43. Ibid.
44. Ibid., 131-132.
45. Henry M. Morris, *Many Infallible Proofs* (El Cajon: Master Books, 1974), 252-255.
46. Ibid.
47. William Lane Craig, *Apologetics: An Introduction* (Chicago: Moody Press, 1984), 88.
48. Ibid., 81-83.
49. Ibid., 81.
50. Ibid., 82.
51. Ibid., 83.
52. Ibid., 83-88.
53. Geisler and Anderson, 138.
54. Graham, 18.
55. Ibid., 12.
56. Norman L. Geisler and Francis Turek, *I Don't Have Enough Faith to Be an Atheist* (Wheaton: Crossway, 2004), 116.
57. Geisler and Anderson, 142.
58. Ibid., 159-164.
59. Abraham Varghese, ed., *Intellectuals Speak Out About God* (Dallas: Lewis and Stanley, 1984), 34. For a thorough refutation of the Miller-Urey experiments see Jonathan Wells, *Icons of Evolution* (Washington, DC: Regnery Publishing, 2000), 9-27.
60. Norman L. Geisler and Winfried Corduan, *Philosophy of Religion* (Grand Rapids: Baker Book House, 1988), 105-106.
61. Geisler and Anderson, 138-139.
62. Ibid., 150-152.

63. Geisler and Turek, 116, 118.
64. Geisler and Anderson, 162.
65. Ibid., 163.
66. Morris, *Many Infallible Proofs*, 256.
67. Ibid.
68. Charles Caldwell Ryrie, *You Mean the Bible Teaches That. .* (Chicago: Moody Press, 1974), 111.
69. Geisler and Anderson, 150.
70. Scott Huse, *The Collapse of Evolution* (Grand Rapids: Baker Book House, 1983), 94.
71. Hugh Ross, *The Creator and the Cosmos* (Colorado Springs: NavPress, 1993), 111-114.
72. Ibid., 129-132.
73. Ibid., 127.
74. Dawkins, *The God Delusion*, 145-147.
75. Ross, *Creator and* Cosmos, 93.
76. Ibid., 92-93.
77. Graham, 75.
78. Ibid.
79. Ibid.
80. Hugh Ross, *The Fingerprint of God* (Orange: Promise Publishing Company, 1991), 53-105.
81. Henry Morris, *Science and the Bible* (Chicago: Moody Press, 1986), 17.
82. Geisler and Anderson, 150-153. For further evidence refuting Darwin's "tree of life" see Wells, *Icons of Evolution*, 41-42.
83. Ibid., 150-152.
84. Louis Agassiz, "Contribution to the Natural History of the United States," *American Journal of Science*, (1860); 144-145.
85. Stephen Jay Gould, "Evolution's Erratic Pace," *Natural History*, (May, 1977); 14.
86. Morris, *Science and the Bible*, 58. For further evidence against the proposed missing links between apes and men, see Wells, *Icons of Evolution*, 209-228.
87. Huse, 98.
88. Morris, *Science and the Bible*, 56.

89. Marvin Lubenow, *Bones of Contention* (Grand Rapids: Baker Book House, 1992), 79.
90. Morris, *Science and the Bible*, 56.
91. Ibid.
92. Ibid., 57-58.
93. Lubenow, 167.
94. Morris, *Science and the Bible*, 58.
95. Ibid.
96. Huse, 110.
97. Morris, *Science and the Bible*, 267-268. See also Huse, 110-112, and Wells, *Icons of* Evolution, 111-135.
98. Huse, 112.
99. Ibid., 44.
100. Geisler and Anderson, 150-153.
101. Ibid.
102. Morris, *Science and the Bible*, 46-47.
103. Ibid.
104. Huse, 120.
105. Ibid., 44.
106. Ibid.

Chapter Four

Is There Evidence for God?

INTRODUCTION

Richard Dawkins and Christopher Hitchens claim that belief in God is irrational, superstitious, and pre-scientific. I disagree. It is my contention, as well as the belief of many others, that not only is belief in God reasonable, but it is more reasonable than atheism.

My case for the existence of a personal, infinite God does not rest on the validity of one sole argument. Instead, I have chosen to utilize a cumulative case for God. This cumulative case will examine nine different aspects of human experience that are more adequately explained by theism (the belief in a personal God) than by atheism (the rejection of the belief in a personal God). The thesis I seek to defend is as follows: it is more reasonable to be a theist than it is to be an atheist.

The God of theism is the eternal uncaused Cause of all else that exists. This Being is personal (i.e., a moral and intelligent being) and unlimited in all His attributes. This Being is separate from His creation (transcendent), but He is also involved with it (immanent).

I will not attempt to prove God's existence beyond all reasonable doubt. Instead, I will merely argue that theism (belief in God) is more reasonable than atheism (the denial of God's existence) when we look at several common aspects of human experience. I am arguing that the preponderance of the evidence favors theism, not atheism. Theism is a more adequate explanation of human experience than the attempted atheistic explanation.

Atheists love to throw rocks at other world views. However, they are rarely willing to go head to head with another world view. It is like a man who lives in a glass house and throws rocks at everyone else's house, but never tells anyone else where he lives, for he fears they will throw rocks at his glass house and destroy it. The atheist enjoys attacking Christianity, rather than defending the supposed strength of his own world view. I challenge Richard Dawkins and Christopher Hitchens to cease from mocking Christianity, and to begin to defend the supposed explanatory power of the atheist world view. If they attempt to do so, the inadequacy of atheism will become evident.

In this chapter, I will look at different aspects of human experience. I will allow theism and atheism to go head to head to see which world view is more plausible. I will argue that theism is far more plausible than atheism.

1) THE BEGINNING OF THE UNIVERSE

This argument is called the kalam cosmological argument for God's existence. Saint Bonaventure utilized this argument.[1] William Lane Craig and J. P. Moreland are two modern proponents of it.[2] This argument is as follows: 1) whatever began to exist must have a cause, 2) the universe began to exist, 3) therefore, the universe had a cause.

Premise #1 uses the law of causality—non-being cannot cause being. In other words, from nothing, nothing comes. Since nothing is nothing, it can do nothing. Therefore, it can cause nothing. Hence, whatever began to exist needs a cause for its existence.

Premise #2 contends that the universe had a beginning. Scientific evidence for the beginning of the universe includes the second law of thermodynamics (energy deterioration) and the Big Bang Model. The second law of thermodynamics is one of the most firmly established laws of modern science. It states that the amount of usable energy in a closed system is running down. This means that someday in the finite future all the energy in the universe will be useless (unless there is intervention from "outside" the universe). In other words, if left to itself, the universe will have an end. But if the universe is going to have an end, it had to have a beginning. At one time, in the finite past, all the energy in the universe was usable. Since the universe is winding down, it must have been wound up. The universe is not eternal; it had a beginning. Since it had a beginning, it needs a cause, for from nothing, nothing comes.

It should also be noted that, due to energy deterioration, if the universe is eternal it would have reached a state of equilibrium in which no change is possible an infinite amount of time ago. All of the universe's energy would already have been used up. Obviously, this is not the case. Therefore, the universe had a beginning.

The Big Bang Model also indicates that the universe had a beginning. In 1929, astronomer Edwin Hubble discovered that the universe is expanding at the same rate in all directions. As time moves forward the universe is growing apart. But this means that if we go back in time the physical universe would get smaller and smaller. Eventually, if we go back far enough in the past, the entire universe would be what scientists call "a point of infinite density" or "a point of dimensionless space." However, if something physical is infinitely dense, it is non-existent, for physical, existent things can only be finitely small. The same can be said for points of dimensionless space. If a physical point has no dimensions, it is non-existent for it takes up no space. Therefore, if the Big Bang Model is correct, it shows that the universe began out of nothing a finite time ago.

There have been two main attempts to refute the beginning of the universe. The first is called the steady-state model. This view holds that the universe never had a beginning. Instead, it always existed in the same state. Because of the mounting evidence for the Big Bang Model, this view has been abandoned my most of its adherents.

The second attempt to evade the beginning of the universe is called the oscillating model. This model teaches that, at some point during the universe's expansion, gravity will halt the expansion and pull everything back together again. From that point there will be another big bang. This process will be repeated over and over again throughout all eternity. However, the oscillating model fails. First, there is no known principle of physics that would reverse the collapse of the universe and cause another big bang. Second, current scientific research has shown that the universe is not dense enough for gravity to pull it back together again. And third, even if it could be proven that several big bangs have occurred, the second law of thermodynamics would still require that there was a first big bang.

Many scientists accept the beginning of the universe, but believe that it does not need a cause. The evidence proposed by these scientists consists of speculation dealing with quantum physics (the study of subatomic particles). Appeal is made to Heisenberg's Principle of Indeterminacy in order to claim that quantum particles pop into existence out of nothing, entirely without a cause. However, Heisenberg's Principle does not necessitate such an absurd interpretation. Simply because scientists cannot presently find the causes does not mean that the causes do not exist. All that Heisenberg's Principle states is that scientists are presently unable to accurately predict where a specific subatomic particle will be at a given time. If this principle proved that events can occur without causes then this would destroy one of the pillars of modern science—the principle of causality (every event must have an adequate cause). It seems obvious to me that the principle of causality is on firmer epistemological ground than the belief that things can pop into existence without a cause.

Non-being cannot cause being. If the universe had a beginning, then it needs a cause. Besides this scientific evidence there is also philosophical evidence for the beginning of the universe. If the universe is eternal, then there would be an actual infinite number of events in time. However, as Zeno's paradoxes have shown, it is impossible to traverse an actual infinite set of points. If we assume the existence of an infinite amount of actual points between two locations, then we can never get from location A to location B, since no matter how many points we have traversed, there will still be an infinite number of points left. If the universe is eternal, then there must exist an actual infinite set of events in the past, but then it would be impossible to reach the present moment. Since the present moment has been reached, there cannot be an actual infinite set of events in the past. There could only be a finite number. Therefore, there had to be a first event. Hence, the universe had a beginning.

It should also be noted that if it is possible for an actual infinite set to exist outside of a mind, contradictions and absurdities would be generated. To illustrate this point, let us look at two infinite sets. Set A consists of all numbers, both odd and even. Set B contains only all the odd numbers. Set A and Set B are equal since they both have an infinite number of members. Still, Set A has twice the number of members as Set B since Set A contains both odd and even numbers, while Set B contains only odd numbers. It is a clear contradiction to say that Set A and Set B have an equal amount of members, while Set A has twice as many members as Set B. Therefore, actual infinite sets cannot exist outside the mind. Actual sets existing outside the mind can only be potentially infinite, not actually infinite. These sets can be added to indefinitely; still, we will never reach an actual infinite by successive addition. Therefore, the universe cannot have an infinite number of events in the past. The universe had a beginning.

Since the universe had to have a beginning, it had to have a cause. For from nothing, nothing comes. But if the universe needs a cause, what if the cause of the universe also needs a cause? Could we not have an infinite chain of causes and effects stretching backwards in time throughout all eternity? Obviously, the answer is no, for we have already shown that an actual infinite set existing outside of a mind is impossible. Therefore, an infinite chain of causes and effects is also impossible. There had to be a first uncaused Cause of the universe. This uncaused Cause would be eternal, without beginning or end. Only eternal and uncaused existence can ground the existence of the universe.

In short, there are only four possible explanations as to why the universe exists. First, the universe could be an eternal chain of causes and effects. Second, the universe could have popped into existence out of nothing without a cause. Third, the universe could merely be an illusion. And, fourth, the universe could have been caused to come into existence by an eternal, uncaused Cause (i.e., God). I have provided strong evidence against the first and second options, as well as strong argumentation in favor of the fourth option. The third option is not a viable position, since it cannot be affirmed without contradiction. Those who claim the universe is an illusion usually contend that all of reality is one mind. However, the communicating of this view necessitates and assumes the existence of two or more minds. Hence, the statement that the universe is an illusion is self-refuting. Therefore, the most plausible explanation for the existence of the universe is that is has an uncaused Cause.

Today, most knowledgeable atheists acknowledge that the universe had a beginning. Still, they argue that the universe did not have a cause—it popped into existence, out of nothing, totally without a cause. "In the beginning God created the universe" seems much more plausible then "In the beginning nothing created the universe." Atheists used to argue, before Hubble showed the universe is expanding, that the universe is eternal, it had no beginning, and hence it doesn't need a cause. Now, atheists admit the universe had a beginning, but still argue that it doesn't need a cause. However, this seems highly improbable. In fact, it is impossible, for no possibility can exist without something actual existing. It makes sense to say that if something actual exists (i.e., God), then He could have had the potential to create. But, if absolutely nothing exists, it (i.e., nothing) had no potential or power to create. Only actual things have potential or power;

nothing lacks the potential to create, or do anything else for that matter. Since the universe had a beginning, theism (belief in God) is more reasonable than atheism.

Therefore, since the universe had a beginning, it must have had an uncaused Cause. Several attributes of the uncaused Cause of the universe can be discovered through examination of the universe. Intelligent life exists in the universe. Since intelligence is a perfection found in the universe, the ultimate Cause of the universe must also be an intelligent Being, for intelligence cannot come from non-intelligence. No one has ever presented a reasonable explanation as to how intelligence could evolve from mindless nature.

Morality also exists in the universe, for without morality, there would be no such thing as right and wrong. However, the moral judgments we make show that we do believe there are such things as right and wrong. Still, nature is non-moral. No one holds a rock morally responsible for tripping him. There is no way that mere "molecules in motion" could produce moral values. Since nature is non-moral but morality exists in the universe, the Cause of the universe must be a moral Being.

The moral law is not invented by individuals, for one individual condemns the actions of another. If morality is relative and subjective, then no one could call the actions of Adolph Hitler wrong. Nor could society be the cause of moral laws, since societies often pass judgment on one another (America and the Allies denounced the actions of Nazi Germany). Even world consensus fails to qualify for the source of moral values since the world consensus once held slavery to be morally defensible. Only an absolute moral Lawgiver who is qualitatively above man can be the Cause of a moral law that stands above man and judges his actions. This moral Lawgiver must be eternal and unchanging since we make moral judgments about the past (slavery, evil treatment of women). Therefore, the uncaused Cause of the universe must be an intelligent, moral Being. This means that God must be a personal Being.

Dawkins refuses to accept any supernatural Cause for the universe. Hence, he is willing to believe in "chance" as the cause of the universe. However, there is a problem with this kind of reasoning. For, if absolutely nothing existed before the beginning of the universe, then chance did not exist as well. For there are no possibilities (i.e., chance) if there is nothing actual. I believe that if a person is willing to go where the evidence leads, then he will conclude that belief in God as the cause of the universe is more plausible than belief in "chance."

The belief that God created the universe is far more believable than the belief that the universe came into existence totally without a cause. It is either "In the beginning God created the heavens and the earth," or "In the beginning nothing created the heavens and the earth." The former is far more plausible than the latter. Concerning the origin of the universe, theism (belief in God) is more reasonable than atheism (the denial of God's existence).

2) THE CONTINUING EXISTENCE OF THE UNIVERSE

This argument for God's existence derives its substance from Thomas Aquinas' five ways to prove God's existence.[3] Experience shows us that limited, dependent (contingent) beings exist. These limited, dependent beings need other beings for their continued existence. For example, I depend on air, water, and food to sustain my existence. However, adding limited, dependent beings will never give us an independent and unlimited whole. Therefore, the sum total of limited, dependent beings is itself limited and dependent. (If each individual part of a floor is wood, then the whole floor will be wood. Likewise, if each part of the universe is dependent, then the entire universe is dependent.) Hence, the ultimate Cause of the continuing existence of all limited, dependent beings must be unlimited and independent (i.e., a Necessary Being).

Here is another way of stating this argument. If everything that exists has the possibility of not existing, then, given enough time, nothing will exist. For, given enough time, every possibility will be actualized. But, this also means that if we were to go backwards in time, eventually we would reach a point in which the same situation would have obtained. Again, nothing would exist. But, since from nothing, nothing comes, something must have always existed with no possibility of non-existence in order to ground the continued existence of all beings that have the possibility of non-existence. The Christian believes God to be this Necessary Being, a being with no possibility of non-existence. This Necessary Being is by definition unlimited and totally independent.

There cannot be two or more unlimited and independent beings since, if there were, they would limit one another's existence, but then they would not be unlimited. Therefore, there can only be one unlimited and independent Being. Also, for two beings to differ, one of the beings would have to have something the other being lacks, or lack something the other being has. This also shows that there cannot be two or more unlimited beings. For a Being to be unlimited, it has to have every possible perfection and must have each of these perfections to an unlimited degree. But, for another being to differ from this unlimited Being, it would have to lack at least one of the perfections or have at least one of the perfections to a less than unlimited degree. But, then this being that differs from the unlimited Being would not itself be unlimited. Again, only one unlimited Being can exist—there cannot be two or more unlimited Beings.

This unlimited Being must have all its attributes in an unlimited way. Otherwise, it would not be an unlimited Being. This Being must be all-powerful, for He is the source of all the power in the universe. No other power can limit Him. He is eternal for He is not limited by time. He is everywhere present since He is not limited by space. He is immaterial since He is not limited by matter. This Being must be all-good since He is not limited by evil. He must also be all-knowing since He is not limited by ignorance.

Since mindless nature works towards goals (such as acorns always becoming oak trees and not something else), there must be an intelligent Designer overseeing natural processes. Without intelligent design, nature's processes would be left to chance. There would be no orderly patterns that could be described as natural laws. Therefore, this infinite and independent Being, whom all finite and dependent beings depend upon for their continued existence, must be an intelligent Being.

Not only does Dawkins invoke "chance" to explain the beginning of the universe, but he also appeals to "chance" to explain the continuing existence of the universe. It is, in my opinion (as well as the opinion of most people), more reasonable to believe that God causes the continuing existence of all the limited beings that exist, than it is to believe that limited beings continue to exist by random chance.

3) THE DESIGN & ORDER FOUND IN THE UNIVERSE

The order, design, and complexity found in the universe strongly imply that the universe is not a random, chaotic throwing together of atoms; rather, it is the product of intelligent design. And, as the product of intelligent design, it necessitates the existence of an intelligent Designer.

Contemporary scientists have found numerous evidences for design in the universe.[4] A few examples will suffice. First, the slightest variation in the expansion rate of the universe would render the universe incapable of sustaining life. Second, British scientists Hoyle and Wickramasinghe estimated that the chances of life evolving from the random shuffling of organic molecules is virtually zero. They calculated that there is only one chance in ten to the twentieth power to form a single enzyme, and just one chance in ten to the forty-thousandth power to produce the approximately 2,000 enzymes that exist. However, Hoyle and

Wickramasinghe point out that the production of enzymes is only one step in the generation of life. Therefore, they concluded there must be some type of Cosmic Intelligence to explain the origin of life.[5] Hoyle compared the probability of life spontaneously generating from non-life as equivalent to the chances of a tornado producing a Boeing 747 from a junkyard.[6]

The cell is the basic unit of life. The DNA molecule of a single-celled animal contains enough complex information to fill one-thousand complete sets of encyclopedia.[7] An explosion in a print shop will never produce one volume of an encyclopedia. That amount of information necessitates an intelligent cause. Also, the human brain contains more genetic information than the world's largest libraries.[8] There is no way that this amount of information could be produced by mere chance. Intelligent intervention is needed.

Third, astrophysicist Hugh Ross listed twenty-five narrowly defined parameters that the universe had to have in order for life to be possible.[9] Ross also pointed out thirty-two narrowly defined parameters for life concerning the earth, its moon, its sun, and its galaxy.[10] For instance, if the distance between the earth and the sun was to differ by just two percent in either direction, no life on earth would be possible.[11] These parameters for life on earth clearly show evidence of design and purpose. Scientists refer to this as the "anthropic principle" (from the Greek word "anthropos" for man) because the universe seems to have been fine-tuned for the purpose of supporting human life on the planet earth.

The theistic hypothesis of intelligent design is obviously more plausible than the atheistic hypothesis of random chance. Even Dawkins admits that the universe has the appearance of being designed. But, then he calls design an "illusion" and speculates about multiple, non-observable universes. Again, he invokes chance. However, if the universe appears as if it was designed, then it is more plausible to believe that it was designed and not the product of blind chance. Science begins with the world of appearances, not wild speculation about non-observable universes. Dawkins' multiverse theory is closer to science fiction than to good science. Whenever there is evidence for a supernatural cause, he invokes all-powerful chance to save the day. This is not evidence against God; rather, it is evidence of Dawkins' flight from God and refusal to accept any evidence for God. It is an explaining away of the scientific evidence—it is not an acceptance of the scientific evidence.

4) THE POSSIBILITY OF HUMAN KNOWLEDGE

The theist claims to know something (i.e., that God exists), and the atheist claims to know something (i.e., that God does not exist). Even the agnostic claims to know something (i.e., that the supposed evidence for God's existence is insufficient). However, it seems to me that only theism (the belief in a personal God) justifies the possibility of human knowledge. For instance, Immanuel Kant argued that man could only know reality as it appeared to him and not reality as it is. Atheism and agnosticism offer no good reason why we should assume that the gap between reality and appearance can be bridged. However, theism entails the doctrine that a rational God created man in His image (i.e., a rational being) and a coherent universe so that through reason man could find out about the universe in which he lives. Remove the rational God of theism from the equation, and the basis for human knowledge appears to crumble. It is hard to imagine how human knowledge and reasoning ability could have evolved into existence from non-rational matter. Again, theism is more rational than atheism.

5) THE REALITY OF UNIVERSAL, UNCHANGING TRUTHS

The denial of absolute truth is self-refuting, for if the statement "there is no absolute truth" is true, then it would be an absolute truth. Complete agnosticism is also self-refuting, for to say that man cannot know truth is a claim to know this "truth." Therefore, there is absolute truth and it is possible for man to know truth.

Some truths are universal, unchanging, and eternal. An example of this would be the mathematical truth "1 + 1 = 2." We do not invent mathematical truths—we discover them. This also applies to the laws of logic (the law of non-contradiction, the law of excluded middle, the law of identity, etc.). These truths stand above human minds and judge human minds. For instance, if we add 1 + 1 and we conclude with 3, the eternal truth that 1 + 1 = 2 will declare us wrong. However, Augustine argued that it is not likely that human, fallible minds are the ultimate cause of universal, unchanging, eternal truths. Augustine concluded that an unchanging, eternal Mind must be the ultimate source of these truths.[12]

Atheism has no basis for eternal, unchanging truths. If atheism is "true," then there may have been a time when 1 + 1 equaled 3. There may also have been a time when torturing innocent babies was good. In fact, if atheism is true, there may have been a time when the statement "God exists" was true.

Atheism implies that there is no truth. Hence, if atheism is true, then it cannot be true, for there is no such thing as truth. Therefore, the existence of truth is more plausible in a theistic universe than in a world without God. The new atheists pride themselves in knowing the truth. Yet, their world view has no place for truth. When the atheist believes in truth it is because he is borrowing capital from the Christian world view. Truth is rather strange furniture for a universe without God.

6) THE EXISTENCE OF ABSOLUTE MORAL LAWS

We all make moral value judgments when we call the actions of another person wrong. When we do this, we appeal to a moral law. This moral law could not originate with each individual, for then we could not call the actions of another person, such as Adolph Hitler, wrong.

The moral law is not a creation of each society, for then one society cannot call the actions of another society, such as Nazi Germany, wrong. The moral law does not come from a world consensus, for world consensus is often mistaken. The world once thought that the earth was flat, the sun revolved around the earth, and slavery was morally acceptable. Appealing to society or world consensus will never give us an adequate cause for the moral law and the moral judgments we make. Appealing to society or world consensus only quantitatively adds men and women. What we need is a moral law qualitatively above man. This moral law must be eternal and unchanging so that we can condemn the actions of the past (i.e., slavery, the holocaust, etc.).

The moral law qualitatively above man is not descriptive of the way things are (as is the case with natural laws). The moral law must be prescriptive—it describes the way things ought to be.[13] Prescriptive laws need a Prescriber. Therefore, a moral Lawgiver must exist, and this Lawgiver must be eternal and unchanging.

We are accountable to this moral Lawgiver that stands above all mankind. Atheist Sigmund Freud failed miserably in his attempt to explain the universal experience of guilt.[14] I believe that the best explanation for the guilt we all experience is the fact that we know we stand guilty before a righteous and holy God. Therefore, when we make moral value judgments, whether it involves self-judgment (a guilty conscience) or judgment of another person, we appeal to a transcendent objective moral law. This is a strong indication that there exists a transcendent moral Lawgiver.

Therefore, theism is a more plausible explanation for our moral experience than atheism is. In fact, the new atheists are very inconsistent when they pronounce moral value judgments against Christianity, since they have no real basis within their atheism for morality.

7) THE ABSURDITY OF LIFE WITHOUT GOD

Each of us thirsts for something more; life on earth never fully satisfies. It is my contention that only the God of the Bible can fully satisfy man's deepest needs. What hope can an atheist offer mankind? People on their deathbeds don't usually call an atheist to comfort them-normally a preacher or a priest is summoned. Even if an atheist could guarantee us seventy years of happiness, what good would that be when compared with the eternity of non-existence that follows? If there is no God who sits enthroned, then Hitler will not be punished for his evil deeds, and Mother Theresa will not be rewarded for her generous works of charity. If there is no God, then a million years from now what would it matter if you were a Hitler or a Mother Theresa? What difference would it make?

Does life have any ultimate meaning if there is no God? If nonexistence is what awaits us, can we really make sense of life? You live and then you die. There are no eternal consequences. Hitler and Mother Theresa have the same destiny. We all finish our meaningless journeys in total nothingness. The famous atheist Bertrand Russell wrote:

> That man is the product of causes which had no prevision of the end they were achieving; that his origin, his growth, his hopes and fears, his loves and his beliefs, are but the outcome of accidental collocations of atoms; that no fire, no heroism, no intensity of thought and feeling, can preserve an individual life beyond the grave; that all the labors of the ages, all the devotion, all the inspiration, all the noonday brightness of human genius, are destined to extinction in the vast death of the solar system, and that the whole temple of man's achievement must inevitably be buried beneath the debris of a universe in ruins . . .[15]

Immediately following this statement, Russell referred to his atheistic philosophy as "the firm foundation of unyielding despair."[16] Without God, life is without meaning.

However, if there is a God, then there is hope. The God of the Bible guarantees the defeat of evil and the triumph of good. He guarantees that Hitler will receive his punishment and Mother Theresa will receive her reward. God gives life meaning, for how we choose to live our lives on earth brings eternal consequences. God is our reason to be optimistic about the future. Only He can overcome our fear of death; only He can defeat evil. Without God, meaningless existence is all we face. Without God, there is no hope.

Without belief in God and life after death, atheism fails to supply man with the necessary ingredients for meaningful existence. Yet, most people live like life has meaning. Again, theism is more reasonable than atheism. The new atheists live like life is meaningful; they act as if their hard work will have lasting effects. They act as if the books they write are worth the trouble. They do not act like they believe that someday the universe will die and everything they ever accomplished will die with it. Without realizing it, they act as if theism is true.

8) RESPECT FOR HUMAN LIFE

If atheism is true, then man is mere molecules in motion. He has no greater value than the animals. In fact, human life would be no more sacred than the existence of a rock. Yet, we act as if human life has more value than the life of animals or the existence of rocks. If the material universe is all there is, then man is just a material part of the universe. There seems to be no basis from which to argue for human rights or the sanctity of human life. Even our founding fathers (who were not always consistent with their ideals) grounded their view of unalienable human rights in their belief that "all men are created equal." I propose that the most reasonable explanation for our common conception of human rights is the biblical teaching that human life has value since we were created in God's image.

Atheism offers no real foundation for human rights. It must again borrow from the Christian world view to posit human rights. Or, the atheist might believe that human rights are man-made—they come from human governments. But, this is probably not a good move for the atheist to make. Research has shown that human government is the number one serial killer of all time, killing well over 100 million innocent people in the twentieth century alone.[17] This is more deaths than have occurred in all of mankind's wars throughout history. Grounding human rights in human government is not a good idea. Human governments did not invent human rights; human rights come from God. God instituted human governments to protect our God-given human rights. If the new atheists have their way, human governments will be able to arbitrarily invent or remove human rights—we will be at the mercy of an all-powerful state. This did not work in the Soviet Union or Red China; it will not work in America either.

9) THE EXISTENCE OF EVIL (ITS CAUSE & ULTIMATE DEFEAT)

Atheists often argue that the existence or amount of evil in the world disproves the existence of the God of the Bible. I see two difficulties with this view. These difficulties cause the argument against God's existence from evil to backfire into an argument for God's existence.[18]

The first difficulty is that the atheist has no explanation for evil within his world view. If the atheist accepts the existence of evil, he must define what it is. If he denies the existence of evil, then he has no basis upon which to call any action evil. Evil can be defined as the perversion or corruption of that which is good.

65

However, for good to be objectively real its existence must be grounded in something ultimately good. In other words, if the atheist acknowledges the existence of evil, his argument dissolves into a moral argument for God's existence. If he denies the existence of evil, his world view is morally bankrupt. If the atheist chooses to accept the existence of evil, but not seek its ultimate cause, then atheism becomes a non-explanation of evil. Hypotheses that do not attempt to explain the data in question should be abandoned. It is not enough to say that evil is "just there."

The second difficulty with the atheistic argument from the problem of evil is the fact that, if evil exists, atheism offers absolutely no solution to the problem. After a life of suffering and pain, people die and cease to exist. Eventually, the entire universe will cease to exist. I believe that the Christian solution to the problem of evil (the death, resurrection, and return of Christ) is the only hope that evil will be defeated. In fact, if Christianity is true, then Christianity guarantees the ultimate defeat of evil. The injustices of this life will be rectified in the hereafter. If atheism is true, death and extinction is the fate of all.

10) HUMAN FREE WILL AND RESPONSIBILITY

If atheism is true then it makes sense that the material world is all that exists. Non-material entities are rather strange furniture for a universe void of God. The physical realm would be all that exists. This would mean that humans do not have immaterial souls. Our choices would not really be free choices; instead, our decisions would merely be chemical reactions occurring in our brains. But, if this is the case, then our choices are biologically determined—we are not free to choose our actions.

If atheistic materialism is true, then we could not hold people responsible for their actions. Someone's brain makes them serve others; another person's brain makes them slaughter others.

Neither person is responsible for their choices or actions. If atheists really believe their world view is correct, then they should fight to close our prisons and set the prisoners free. For if human free will is an illusion (and consistent atheism says it is), then criminals are not responsible for their actions and therefore should not be punished for their actions. But, most atheists want to see criminals behind bars—they live like Christianity is true; they live like man is free and he is responsible for the choices he makes. Again, the theistic explanation is more plausible than the attempted atheistic explanation.

11) SELF-AWARENESS

Hitchens and Dawkins ridicule people for believing in God. Yet, it is Hitchens and Dawkins who are guilty of blind, naïve faith—not the Christian. It is Hitchens and Dawkins who ask us to trust them and blindly believe that self-awareness evolved into existence by chance. It stretches credulity to believe that chance plus time plus natural laws plus matter somehow accidently produced beings who are aware of their own existence! Most people disagree with the new atheists—they believe that a self-aware Being (i.e., God) created humans (with or without using evolution) in His image as self-aware beings. It makes more sense to believe that our self-awareness comes from a self-aware Being than from non-conscious matter through chance. No matter how much time is available, chance will never produce self-aware beings from mere matter.

12) FEELINGS OF GUILT

We all experience guilt when we do wrong, even if we sin when no one else is looking. Guilt is our innate knowledge of good and evil informing us that we have done evil. Even atheists experience guilt. They try to explain it away rather than admit that guilt tells us we have sinned before a holy God. One of the most famous atheists of all time—Sigmund Freud—devoted much of his thought and writing in an attempt to provide a naturalistic explanation of guilt. His wild speculation suggested that the first tribe of human males murdered their father due to their desire to have sex with their mothers. After killing their father, they felt guilty. Freud never actually explains why they felt guilty—the question as to why humans experience guilt remains. It seems more likely that we experience guilt because we really are guilty. We have sinned before a holy God, and we need His deliverance. Guilt is a very strange piece of furniture in the universe if no God exists. Theism offers a far more plausible explanation for guilt than does atheism.

CONCLUSION

In the famous debate on the existence of God between Bertrand Russell and Frederick Copleston, the atheist Bertrand Russell stated concerning the existence of the universe, "I should say that the universe is just there, and that's all."[19] It is my contention that atheism fails as an explanation of significant aspects of human experience, and that theism is a more reasonable hypothesis. If the atheist could say that "the universe is just there," could he not say that moral laws, design and order, universal truths, the human experience of guilt, the sanctity of human life, the possibility of human knowledge, and meaning in life are "just there" as well. To avoid looking for an explanation is not the same thing as the search for an explanation. In this sense, the theistic explanation is superior to the atheistic explanation, for the latter reduces to a non-explanation.

However, the atheist may choose to deny the reality of moral laws, design and order, universal truths, the human experience of guilt, the sanctity of human life, the possibility of human knowledge, and meaning in life. If the atheist takes this strategy, my response is that he can't live consistently with the view that these things are not real. Even the atheist lives as if some things are wrong and other things are right. He lives as if human life is sacred, and life has meaning.

Rational statements only make sense within some type of rational context. The atheist, by arguing against God's existence, has removed the rational context (the universe as an effect of the rational God) for rational discourse. He reasons against God; but if there is no God, there is no reason.

Is it reasonable to believe that the universe popped into existence out of absolute nothingness—entirely without a cause? Or, is it rational to conclude that the universe is eternal despite the strong scientific and philosophical evidences that indicate that the universe had a beginning? Is the atheist justified in holding to the idea that time plus chance plus natural laws worked upon "primordial soup" until it eventually birthed a French philosopher who declared, "I think, therefore I am"? If atheism is true, then, given enough time, that's what occurred! (Atheistic evolution only appears plausible in slow motion. Duane Gish stated that when we hear about a frog instantly becoming a prince, we call it a fairy tale. But if we are told that a frog became a prince gradually over a period of several million years, we call this science.)

From molecules in motion will never come moral values or the laws of logic. From a mound of dirt, a single thought will never be produced—no matter how much time is given. Chance plus time plus natural laws will never produce self-awareness or guilt. If no God exists and all we are is mere molecules in motion, from whence come human rights? If an innocent child is merely a random collection of atoms, can we really say that it is wrong to crush him? If there is no life after death and all we face is everlasting extinction, can this life really have meaning? What counsel can an atheist offer a suffering friend on his deathbed? Can we climb above despair if all we face is extinction? When the universe dies, all will die with it. If atheism is true, then human experience is a cruel joke. And, if life is a cruel joke, then why even bother to go on living? If there is no lasting hope for the future, they why pretend there is hope?

I do not believe that we can prove God's existence with rational certainty. However, I believe that the theistic explanation is far superior to the atheistic explanation. The God of theism is an all-good God who eternally rewards those who earnestly seek Him. Either this type of God exists or He does not exist. I beseech you to choose this God, for, as the Christian thinker and scientist, Blaise Pascal, has said, if you choose God and lose, you lose nothing. But, if you choose God and He exists, you win eternity. Pascal also pointed out that if you choose against God and He does not exist, you gain nothing, but if you choose against God and He does exist, you lose everything. Therefore, the wise man will choose God.[20]

We have nothing to gain and everything to lose if we join Christopher Hitchens and Richard Dawkins by wagering our lives that God does not exist. This point is magnified when we realize that belief in God is a more reasonable explanation than atheism is for the common aspects of human experience that we have discussed. There are good reasons for believing in God. In fact, it is more reasonable to believe in God than it is to deny His existence.

ENDNOTES

1. Copleston, *A History of Philosophy*, vol. 2, 262-265.
2. William Lane Craig, *Reasonable Faith* (Wheaton: Crossway Books, 1994), 91-122. J. P. Moreland, Scaling the Secular City (Grand Rapids: Baker Book House, 1987), 22-42.
3. Thomas Aquinas, *Summa Theologiae*, 1a. 2,3.
4. J. P. Moreland and Kai Nielsen, *Does God Exist? The Great Debate* (Nashville: Thomas Nelson Publishers, 1990), 35-36.
5. Ibid., 143.
6. Ibid., 35.
7. Norman L. Geisler and J. Kerby Anderson, *Origin Science* (Grand Rapids: Baker Book House, 1987), 162.
8. Ibid.
9. Hugh Ross, *The Creator and the Cosmos* (Colorado Springs: NavPress, 1993), 111-114.
10. Ibid., 129-132.
11. Ibid., 127.
12. Augustine, *On Free Will*, 2.6.
13. C. S. Lewis, *Mere Christianity* (New York: Collier Books, 1952), 27-28.
14. Ninian Smart, *The Religious Experience of Mankind* (New York: Charles Scribner's Sons, 1976), 40-41.
15. Bertrand Russell, *Why I Am Not a Christian* (New York: Simon and Schuster, 1957), 107.
16. Ibid.
17. R. J. Rummel, *Death by Government* (New Brunswick, NJ: Transaction Publishers, 1997), 9.
18. William Lane Craig, *No Easy Answers* (Chicago: Moody Press, 1990), 99-100.
19. John Hick, ed., *The Existence of God*, 175.
20. Pascal, *Pensees*, 149-155.

Chapter Five

Is Christianity Intolerant?

Does Religion Poison Everything?

The new atheists believe that religion poisons everything. However, they conveniently do not classify atheism as a religion. But, we have shown that atheism is a religion. Whether we like it or not, each society or culture usually shares a dominant world view or religion. And the government of that society is influenced by that world view or religion. Sometimes, however, power hungry individuals take over a government and force their world view or religion on the masses who favor a different religion or world view. Whatever the case, religion (even the atheistic religion) has a significant impact on government.

Though we have all heard the liberal rallying cry of "separation of church and state," the fact of the matter is this: human government cannot exist in a spiritual vacuum. Human government must be based upon certain presuppositions about man and the universe in which he lives. In short, political and economic theories must be based upon a religious foundation. Thomas Jefferson, the author of *the Declaration of Independence*, recognized this when he penned the words, "all men are created equal." Even the atheists who signed the first *Humanist Manifesto* acknowledged man's reliance upon religious ideas by stating that, "nothing human is alien to the religious."[1] Human beings are incurably religious, and their governments must have a religious foundation as well.

Richard Dawkins and Christopher Hitchens blame traditional religion for much (if not most) of the world's wars and violence. Yet, they exempt atheism from such a criticism. When professing Christian societies persecute others, it is because Christianity is evil and it leads to evil consequences. On the other hand, Dawkins and Hitchens argue that there is no evidence indicating that atheism has led to death and violence. When atheistic communists murder tens of millions, it is despite their atheism, not because of their atheism. At least, this is what the new atheists would have us believe. However, when we examine human history, a different portrait emerges. If Christian societies must answer for the evil done in Christ's name, then atheistic regimes must be held accountable for the genocides they have produced.

We will now look at different religions (including atheism) to determine what kind of impact they have had on their societies. It will become obvious that the Christian world view has a much better track record than that of atheism. Despite the fact that Christians (or at least professing Christians) have done horrible things in the name of Christ, Christianity at its worst is still head and shoulders above atheism due to the atrocities committed in the name of atheism. While Christians disagree with Hitchens' claim that "religion poisons everything," we can agree with the statement "false religion poisons everything." And atheism is one of those false religions. In fact, it is one of the bloodiest of the false religions, a fact attested to by history.

THE JUDEO-CHRISTIAN WORLD VIEW

The United States government was founded upon the Judeo-Christian world view (i.e., the Bible).[2] Our founding fathers believed that all men were created equal and in God's image, and that all men have God-given rights that could not be taken away. God instituted human government to protect these unalienable rights.

According to our founding fathers, the need for human government is twofold. First, because man was created in God's image, human life is sacred and therefore worth protecting. Second, because man is in a fallen and sinful state, human life needs to be protected, for some humans infringe upon the God-given rights of other humans. Thus, the need for human government is based upon the biblical doctrines of Creation and the Fall.

Our founding fathers took seriously the sinfulness of mankind. They recognized that since human governments are ruled by sinful humans, government power must be limited. No man or group of men should be allowed to have their sinful lust for power go unchecked. Our nation's founders heeded Lord Acton's advice—"power corrupts, and absolute power corrupts absolutely." Therefore, *the Declaration of Independence* and the *United States Constitution* limited the power of government officials in several ways. First, God and His laws were recognized as existing above human government and its officials. Government officials are not above the law; they are answerable to God. Second, global government was rejected. A global government limited in power is an oxymoron. Third, a system of checks and balances and separation of powers (federal and state governments & the three branches of the federal government) were established to prevent the unleashing of a unified assault against the American people and their freedoms. Fourth, the people's rights to worship as they saw fit, elect many of their government officials, peacefully protest the government's actions, and bear arms were protected.

Since America was founded on the biblical view of government and morality, the rights of individuals were protected—they were each created in God's image. The biblical teaching of creation has done more for the cause of human rights than any other doctrine.

The Constitution does not force Americans to become Jews or Christians, but, because it is based upon the Judeo-Christian world view, it protects a person's freedom to worship according to the dictates of his or her conscience. The form of government America has and the freedoms we enjoy are due to the Judeo-Christian world view. Our founding fathers acknowledged the biblical view of government and morality in their political and economic thought. Political liberals may not like this fact, but it is a historical fact nonetheless. Although political liberals wish to change the religious presuppositions of our government, the alternatives are not very promising. And we must never forget that governments must have a religious base. We will now look at some of the alternatives to the Judeo-Christian basis for human government.

ATHEISM/SECULAR HUMANISM

In *Humanist Manifestos I and II*, atheist leaders proposed to save this planet by working towards a one-world socialistic government based upon the foundation of the atheistic world view.[3] However, in this century we have witnessed the horrors produced by governments based upon atheism. The totalitarian regimes of the Soviet Union and Red China together have systematically slaughtered more than 80 million of their own people in this century alone.[4] This is more deaths that have occurred in the history of mankind's wars! Dawkins and Hitchens try in vain to distance themselves from the atheist communists who have slaughtered millions in the twentieth century. Dawkins has the audacity to write, "I do not believe there is an atheist in the world who would bulldoze Mecca—or Chartres, York Minster or Notre Dame, the Shwe Dagon, the temples of Kyoto or, of course, the Buddhas of Bamivan."[5] Apparently, he thinks that when atheist tyrants declare war on Christianity or other religions, it has nothing to do with their atheism. Dawkins seriously needs a reality check,

76

for the world view of the old Soviet Union and Red China is hauntingly similar to that of the new atheists. These communist regimes and the new atheists reject belief in God and miracles, accept Darwinian evolution, and oppose religious teaching for children. It is difficult, if not impossible, to find governments founded on a belief system closer to that of Dawkins and Hitchens.

Atheism, by denying belief in God's existence, is a world view that has no basis for the sanctity of human life. Man is merely molecules in motion, having no intrinsic worth. Since atheists also reject a historical Fall of mankind, man's lust for power is left unchecked. A "survival of the fittest" mentality is allowed to run rampant among government leaders. While claiming to have the best interests of the populace in mind, government officials are answerable to no one as they seek to increase their power.

Influential Western atheists have argued for a morality that at times comes dangerously close to the ideas of Hitler's Nazi regime. This is not an overstatement. When God is removed from the universe, man plays God. If God is dead, man is dead as well.

Margaret Sanger, the founder of Planned Parenthood, was an ardent proponent of Darwinian evolution. She promoted eugenics, the belief that "inferior" races should be exterminated through sterilization, abortion, infanticide, and euthanasia.[6] This is consistent with Charles Darwin's views. Darwin, in his work *The Descent of Man*, argued that it is a mistake to allow the weaker members of the human race to reproduce.[7]

B. F. Skinner was a materialist—he believed that only matter exists and that there is no spiritual realm. Hence, he believed human free will, responsibility, and dignity should be eliminated. Skinner promoted an all-powerful State, led by his atheists like colleagues, that would dictate man's every move.[8]

World renowned ethicist Peter Singer of Princeton University argues that healthy individuals should not be forced to keep their unhealthy loved ones alive—they should have the right to euthanize those whose lives are not worthy of living.[9] Rather than the Judeo-Christian principle of the sanctity of human life (i.e., that all human life is sacred), atheists promote the quality of human life, deeming some human life as undesirable.

James Watson and Francis Crick, the scientists who won the Nobel Prize for cracking the genetic code, reject the existence of the God of the Bible. Hence, they believe man is the ultimate authority. They have publicly stated that governments should establish a three day trial period after the birth of a child and not declare the baby alive or human until after the third day. In this way, the doctors and the parents could examine the child and determine whether or not it should live.[10]

Consistent atheism not only entails a rejection of traditional values, but also a complete denial of any absolute moral laws. Therefore, there is no such thing as right and wrong; the end (the goals of those in power) justifies the means (even if millions are slaughtered). Atheism fails to supply the moral foundation necessary for good government. Therefore, if the Judeo-Christian world view is rejected, we must look elsewhere for an alternative religious base for human government.

ISLAM

In the militant Islamic world view of Iran, the government leader (the ayatollah) is viewed as the infallible spokesman for God.[11] This is the Shi'ite branch of Islam. It perverts the Judeo-Christian world view by allowing a sinful man to stand in the place of God. The results can be the same as that of the atheistic world view since the atheist denial of God's existence causes its government leaders to attempt to replace God as the highest authority. The power of the government leader is not held in check. Whenever a human leader (other than the Lord Jesus who is fully God and fully man) stands in the place of God and claims to speak infallibly for God, oppression will almost surely follow. This was seen during the Carter administration when Ayatollah Khomeni took innocent Americans hostage for 444 days. The militant wing of Shi'ite Islam is known as Hezbollah.

The violent side of Islam is not only found in the Shi'ite Islam of Iran, but also in the Sunni Islam of other Muslim countries. Most Muslims in the world are Sunni Muslims. Within the Sunni branch of Islam, two movements deserve our attention. The Wahhabi movement originated in Saudi Arabia in the eighteenth century, and the Deobandi movement began in India in the nineteenth century and is currently popular in Pakistan.[12] Both branches of Sunni Islam are reform movements within the Muslim world. These groups literally interpret the Koran (the Muslim holy book written by Muhammad) and the Hadith (early and authoritative Muslim traditions). Therefore, they take seriously Muhammad's commands to slay the idolaters or infidels (Surah 9:5; 5:34-35, etc.). They often use force and violence to purify the Islamic faith. This entails terrorist attacks on liberal or modern Muslims as well as acts of unprovoked violence against the non-Muslim world. The Al-Qaida terrorist network, the Taliban, and Osama Bin Laden have links with both Deobandi and Wahhabi Islam. The terrorist attacks against America on September 11, 2001 were the work of Bin Laden and his followers.

Though some would argue that violent Muslims, whether of the Shi'ite or Sunni type, are perverting the peaceful and tolerant religion of Islam, the facts tell a different story. Though most Muslims are probably peace-loving people, the Koran and the Hadith call for the slaying of non-Muslims wherever they are found. Muhammad meant Jihad (a holy war fought in the name of Allah, the Muslim God) to be taken literally; he himself conquered non-Muslims with the sword. In fact, whereas the first three centuries of Christianity saw thousands of defenseless Christians persecuted, the first three hundred years of Islam were characterized by Islamic military conquests of non-Muslim lands. Professing Christians who kill innocents in Jesus' name pervert the teachings of Christ; Muslims who commit terrorist acts in the name of Allah are following Muhammad's example and obeying the teachings of Muhammad as found in the Koran as well as the Hadith. A "back to the Bible" movement usually leads to religious freedom, while a "back to the Koran" movement will always lead to bloodshed and violence. It is no coincidence that every government heavily influenced by the Islamic faith offers no religious freedom to non-Muslims. In Middle-Eastern Muslim countries, non-Muslims can be executed for trying to convert a Muslim, and in the Sudan more than 2 million professing Christians have been killed by Muslims since the 1950's.

POLYTHEISM

Many tribal peoples in Africa and South America hold to the belief in many gods, called polytheism. The animism (the belief that all nature is animated with spirits) of American Indians was very similar to polytheism. History has shown that polytheism and animism leave their adherents in occultism, superstition, poverty, and anarchy. Human sacrifice is often practiced (i.e., Incas, Aztecs, Mayas). Polytheism offers no unified code of ethics to unite its people, since the gods are often opposed to one another. Ancient dictators were more than willing to bring in their own unifying principle (usually the enforced worship of the emperor or ruler as the superior god) while using polytheism to aid them in suppressing the rights of their people. In short, polytheism often produces a society that lacks a unified direction, thus making that society easy prey for potential dictators. The finite gods of polytheism are not able to sustain a society.

OTHER-WORLDLY PANTHEISM

Pantheism is the belief that God is the universe, and that, since man is part of the universe, man is God. In India, the society and government are based upon this world view due to India's most popular religion-Hinduism. But this type of Hindu pantheism in India is an *other-worldly* pantheism—the emphasis is not on this life, but on future reincarnations. This lessens the incentive of Hindus to alleviate the suffering of others, for the suffering person is working off negative karma. To alleviate his suffering would be to force him to return to this world, in a different body, and to suffer again to work off the negative karma. Thus, helping alleviate a person's sufferings is viewed as a hindrance to that person's spiritual progress. This is why many of the health care workers in India are Christian (or, at least nominal Hindus).

The caste system in India is another consequence of other-worldly pantheism. It is almost impossible for a person to leave the caste (or class) into which they are born, since the person is thought to be in that caste due to the karma he has brought from a former life. Usually, it is assumed that a future incarnation is the only way for a person to move out of their caste. Due to the other-worldly pantheism of India, suffering people are often neglected since they are thought to be working off negative karma.

It should be noted that any reform movements in India attempting to change the caste system are actually contrary to the doctrines of Hindu Pantheism. On the other hand, reform movements in America, such as the abolition of slavery, were actually bringing American life more in conformity to the Judeo-Christian world view.

THIS-WORLDLY PANTHEISM

In contrast to the other-worldly pantheism of India is the *this-worldly* pantheism of Nazi Germany.[13] In early twentieth century Germany the leadership of the German Church had all but apostatized. In earlier decades, German theologians and philosophers had attacked the authenticity and reliability of the

Bible, causing many professing Christians in Germany to lose their confidence in the traditional Christian world view. The German Volk religion filled the void left by the church's apostasy. It became the dominating religious perspective of Germany's leadership.

The German Volk religion was a pantheistic ideology that held that the Aryan race is divine and that the German leader (Hitler) was the fullest manifestation of the divine. Non-Aryan races were viewed as "sub-human." These races were seen as a threat to human progress, for it was feared that they could pollute the pure genetic make-up of the Aryan (master) race. The emphasis of the pantheism of the German Volk religion was on this life and the supposed future spiritual evolution of the Aryan race. The undesirable "sub-human" races had to be weeded out in order to usher in a "new age" of spiritual enlightenment. Richard Wiekart's research has confirmed that the Nazis utilized Darwinian evolution for the justification of their morality-eugenics, euthanasia, and extermination of the undesriables.[14]

Thus, the holocaust, which took the lives of more than 6 million innocent Jews, was motivated by the this-worldly pantheism of Adolph Hitler and the Third Reich. Hitler's regime also murdered at least an additional 14 million non-Jews. The present-day version of this-worldly pantheism is the New Age Movement. Both the New Age Movement and the German Volk religion were greatly influenced by the occult beliefs of Theosophy, a cult founded by the Russian mystic Helena Blavatsky.[15] The New Age Movement, if it continues to grow in popularity, may produce another holocaust; however, this holocaust may cover the entire earth. New Age leader and author Barbara Marx Hubbard believes that not everyone is ready for the coming New Age of peace and spiritual enlightenment. In fact, she believes that traditional Christians, Jews, and Muslims are holding back the spiritual evolution of mankind because they refuse to acknowledge that man is God. Therefore, reasons Hubbard, one-fourth of mankind needs to be exterminated in order to usher in the New Age.[16]

Pantheism (in both its this-worldly and other-worldly forms) teaches that God is an impersonal force, not the personal God of the Bible. Being an impersonal force, the God of pantheism is beyond the moral categories of right and wrong. Therefore, ultimately, there are no moral absolutes; what is right for one person is not necessarily right for another person, and visa versa. Usually this moral relativistic view translates into a toleration of willful, immoral behavior (i.e., homosexuality, abortion, euthanasia, sexual immorality, pornography, etc.), as well as an inconsistent lack of toleration of traditional values and beliefs (i.e., the Judeo-Christian world view). Unfortunately, that which a this-worldly pantheistic world view cannot tolerate it usually exterminates. For although the concept that man is God appears to be a high view of man, it is actually devalues human life since it entails the weeding out of undesirables who hold back human progress. (For the New Age Movement the undesirables include traditional Christians and Jews, as well as patriotic Americans who hold to traditional values.)

WHAT ABOUT THE INQUISITION AND THE CRUSADES?

Christianity is often blamed for the terrors of the Inquisition and the bloodshed of the Crusades. In reference to the Inquisition, several things need to be clarified. First, the Inquisition was primarily a killing & torturing of those who opposed the Bishop of Rome. In other words, it should not be viewed as an indictment on traditional, protestant Christianity (i.e., Bible-based Christianity). When the church and the Roman Empire merged, it was the empire that corrupted the church, not the other way around. Second, much of the inquisition dealt with torturing and killing Jews merely because they were Jews and they would not convert to "Christianity." But, true Christians cannot hate Jews. Jesus was Jewish. The apostles were Jewish. The Bible (Old and

New Testaments) is Jewish. True Christians pray for Israel and love the Jewish nation since it is God's chosen nation. Jesus said "not everyone who says to Me 'Lord, Lord' shall enter the Kingdom of Heaven, but he who does the will of My Father in heaven" (Matthew 7:21). Third, Bible-believing Christians defend Jesus, not the actions of a fallible church. We do not believe the church is infallible, nor do we believe that the Bishop of Rome (i.e., the Pope) is infallible when he speaks for the entire church in areas of faith or practice. Protestants acknowledge that professing Christians have committed horrors in the name of Christ, but we believe that their actions prove them to be outside the true faith, for "faith without works is dead" (James 2:26). Fourth, during the Inquisition many true Christians were tortured and killed because they refused to submit to the Bishop of Rome. Often, the Inquisition was characterized by professing Christians killing true Bible-believing Christians as well as Jews.

The Crusades involved the waging of war in behalf of the Church of Rome. The early crusades were fought in defense of the Eastern Church as she was being attacked by Muslim invaders. Still, later Crusades morally deteriorated to the point where there is simply no way to justify them. Again, we must remember that these actions were ordered by the Roman Catholic Church. Protestants argue against the church hierarchy having that kind of authority; Protestants reject the notion of papal infallibility. Like the Inquisition, the Crusades show that not all professing believers are genuine Christians.

Having said this, we must acknowledge that every nation (even a so-called Christian nation) has the right to defend itself. We must remember that the Crusades started as a defensive action against Islamic militarism.

In a book entitled *Christianity on Trial*, authors Vincent Carroll and David Shiflett sum up the issue well:

> Whatever Christianity's role in the conflicts of the last two millennia, its hands were clean during the bloodiest

84

century on record—the one just past. The body count from the two great barbarisms of the twentieth century, communism and Nazism, is extraordinary enough on its own. Communism's toll ran to perhaps 100 million . . . Adolph Hitler's death machine was equally efficient, but ran a much shorter course . . . Communism was and is proudly atheistic, while Nazism . . . embraced a form of neo-paganism. Both were hostile to the organized religions in their midst, and neither genuflected before any power other than man himself. Yet these movements exterminated their victims with an efficiency that clearly exceeded the most grisly achievement of states produced by Christian zealotry. In that sense, they were worthy heirs to the French Revolution, which erected altars to the Goddess of Reason before the backdrop of a guillotine.[17]

CONCLUSION

Government cannot be separated from religion. Every government must have a doctrine of man and his place in the universe, and it is here that government and religion overlap. If a government rejects the faith of our founding fathers (the Judeo-Christian world view), then it will accept an alternative world view. But the consequences of that alternative world view will infringe on man's freedom and eventually result in great loss of life, for the dethronement of God is not without consequences. Despite the objections of Richard Dawkins, Christopher Hitchens, and their atheist colleagues, contemporary man's flight from God will inevitably lead him down the dark, bloody road to tyranny.

ENDNOTES

1. Paul Kurtz, ed. *Humanist Manifesto I & II* (Buffalo: Prometheus Books, 1972), 9.

2. It is true that not all of our founding fathers were Christians. Some were deists; they denied the miraculous elements of Christianity. Still, the founding fathers who were deists were *pro-Christian deists*. They were politically conservative and held to the biblical view of government and morality. On the other hand, *anti-Christian deists* could be found among the leaders of the bloody French Revolution. Anti-Christian deists are politically liberal—they believe that big government has all the answers to man's problems, and that man, through his reason, can save this planet. Anti-Christian deists reject the biblical view of limited government as well as the biblical view of morality. Modern deists usually fall into the anti-Christian deist camp. They often have more in common with secular humanists (i.e., atheists) than with adherents of the Judeo-Christian world view.

3. Kurtz, 8, 10, 21.

4. R. J. Rummel, *Death by Government* (New Brunswick: Transaction Publishers, 1994), 8.

5. Richard Dawkins, *The God Delusion* (Boston: Houghton Mifflin, 2006), 249.

6. Margaret Sanger, *The Pivot of Civilization* (Lenox, MA: Hard Press, 2006), 17, 37, 41, 74-75.

7. Charles Darwin, *The Descent of Man, and Selection in Relation to Sex*, with an introduction by John Tyler Bonner and Robert M. May (Princeton: Princeton University press, 1981), Part I, Chapter Five, 168.

8. Francis Schaeffer, *Complete Works*, vol. 1 (Westchester: Crossway Books, 1982), 373-384.

9. Peter Singer, *Practical Ethics*, second edition (Cambridge: Cambridge University Press, 1993), 135-217, 342-343.

10. Francis Schaeffer, *Complete Works*, vol. 5 (Westchester: Crossway Books, 1982), 231-235, 319-320.

11. Timothy Demy and Gary P. Stewart, *In the Name of God* (Eugene: Harvest House Publishers, 2002), 58-59.

12. Ibid., 59-62, 80-82.

13. Richard Terrell, *Resurrecting the Third Reich* (Lafayette: Huntington House Publishers, 1994), 49-61, 145-168.

14. Ibid., 50. Richard Weikart, *From Darwin to Hitler* (New York: Palgrave Macmillan, 2004), 229-233.

15. Ibid., 49, 151-153.

16. Tal Brooke, *One World* (Berkeley: End Run Publishing, 2000), 197. Hubbard is an insider with the United Nations and the United Religions Organization. She is not alone in her thinking. Her idea that a large portion of the world's population needs to be exterminated is shared by Cornell Professor David Pimentel. In 1994, he argued before the American Association for the Advancement of Science that the total population of the world should not exceed 2 billion people. Since the world's current population is about 6 billion, Pimentel apparently would like to see 4 billion people "disappear." Pimentel's wild idea was treated with respect by the *Los Angeles Times*. See William Norman Grigg, *Freedom on the Altar* (Appleton: American Opinion Publishers, 1995), 109.

17. Vincent Carroll and David Shiflett, *Christianity on Trial* (San Francisco: Encounter Books, 2002), 109.

Chapter Six

Does Evil Disprove God?

One of the greatest obstacles keeping people from accepting Christ is the problem of evil.[1] Christopher Hitchens and Richard Dawkins use the existence of evil and human suffering as supposed evidence that God does not exist. The problem of evil is nothing new—great Christian thinkers (i.e., Augustine, Aquinas, etc.) of the past dealt with this objection to Christianity.

The problem of evil can take several different forms. First, the metaphysical problem of evil asks how evil can exist in a world created by an all-good God.[2] Is God the cause of evil, or, is evil itself uncreated and eternal? Maybe evil is not real. Maybe it is simply an illusion.[3] The metaphysical problem deals with the origin and reality of evil in God's universe.

Second, the moral problem of evil deals with the evil choices of personal beings.[4] This form of the problem argues that since an all-good God would want to destroy evil, and an all-powerful God is able to destroy evil, the existence of evil proves that no all-good, all-powerful God exists.[5] The Christian apologist defends the existence of an all-good and all-powerful God. Therefore, he will respond to this argument.

The third form of the problem of evil is called the physical problem of evil.[6] The physical problem of evil deals with incidents of natural disasters and innocent humans suffering.[7] How could God allow evil to occur that is not directly caused by the abuse of human free will?[8]

The fourth and final form of the problem of evil is not really a philosophical issue. It is the personal problem of evil.[9] The personal problem of evil is not a theoretical question about the existence of evil. Instead, it is a personal struggle with a traumatic experience in one's own life.[10] Examples of this would be the sudden and unexpected death of a loved one, a bitter divorce, the loss of a job, or the like. In these situations, the troubled person does not need philosophical answers. What is needed is encouragement, comfort, and biblical counsel.[11] Since this form of the problem of evil does not deal with philosophical discussion, it will not be dealt with in this chapter. The remainder of this chapter will deal with the first three forms of the problem of evil.

THE METAPHYSICAL PROBLEM OF EVIL

The metaphysical problem of evil can be stated as follows: 1) God created everything that exists, 2) evil exists, 3) therefore, God created evil.[12] There are several ways people respond to this argument. First, like the Christian Science Cult, some choose to deny the reality of evil.[13] They view evil as an illusion, but this entails a rejection of Christian Theism which clearly accepts the real existence of evil and offers Christ as its solution.[14] Therefore, viewing evil as an illusion is not an option for the Christian apologist.

A second possible response to the metaphysical problem is dualism. This is the view that God and evil are coeternal.[15] In this view, God did not create evil since evil is eternal. This view fails in that it makes evil a second ultimate being along with God. God would then no longer be infinite since He and evil would limit each other. However, the cosmological argument has shown that there must be an infinite Being to explain and ground all finite existence. There cannot be two infinite beings, for they would limit each other. If God and evil are both finite, then there would have to be an infinite cause for the existence of both. Dualism would only

90

push the problem of evil further back. It does not offer any ultimate solution to the dilemma. Also, the acceptance of dualism entails a rejection of the existence of the God of the Bible. Therefore, it is not an option for the Christian theist.[16]

The Christian apologist must defend the reality of evil without proposing evil as eternal or as a creation of God.[17] Saint Augustine dealt with this same problem centuries ago. His proposed solution to the metaphysical problem of evil was that all things created by God are good. Nothing in its created nature is evil. Evil, therefore, cannot exist solely on its own. However, evil is real; it does exist. Still, it must exist in something good. Evil is a privation, a lack or absence of a good that should be there. Evil is a corruption or perversion of God's good creation. Blindness in a man is evil, for God created man to see. But, blindness in a rock is not evil, for God never meant rocks to have sight. Evil, according to Augustine, is a lack of a good that should be there. Augustine stated, "evil has no positive nature; what we call evil is merely the lack of something that is good."[18]

Augustine stated that God did not create evil; He merely created the possibility for evil by giving men and angels free will. When men and angels exercised their free will by disobeying God, they actualized the possibility for evil.[19]

Thomas Aquinas argued against the metaphysical problem of evil along the same lines as did Augustine.[20] This basic response has been the traditional Christian solution to the metaphysical problem of evil. God did not create evil, but, evil exists as a privation or corruption of that which is good. God cannot be blamed for evil. He is only responsible for creating the possibility of evil. When God gave angels and men free will, He created the possibility of evil. Fallen angels and fallen men are responsible for evil through their abuse of free will.[21]

THE MORAL PROBLEM OF EVIL

The moral problem of evil affirms that an all-good God would want to destroy evil, while an all-powerful God is able to destroy evil. Since evil exists, it is concluded that an all-good, all-powerful God does not exist.[22] Some people respond by denying God's existence (atheism). Others deny that God is all-powerful (finite godism). Rabbi Harold Kushner is an example of the latter. He argues that God is not all-powerful. Kushner declares that mankind needs to forgive God for His failures and help Him to combat evil.[23] Obviously, the options of atheism and finite godism are not viable for Christians. Christians must defend both God's omnipotence (all-powerfulness) and His infinite goodness. Therefore, the moral problem of evil must be answered in another way. Christian philosophers Geisler and Corduan offer several effective responses to the moral problem of evil.

First, there is an unnecessary time limit placed on God.[24] The argument against the existence of the theistic God from moral evil assumes that because evil exists God cannot be both all-good and all-powerful. However, what if an all-good and all-powerful God allowed evil for the purpose of a greater good? What if this God is also in the process of destroying evil and will someday complete the process?[25]

Second, God may have created the possibility of evil for the purpose of a greater good (human and angelic free will). God would not force His love on angels or mankind, for any attempt to force love on another is rape (and not really love at all).[26] Therefore, He gave men and angels the freedom to accept or reject His love and His will. Free will necessitates the possibility of evil coming into the universe.[27] In fact, human and angelic free choices brought evil and human suffering into the world.

Third, God will use evil for good purposes. If evil did not exist, there could be no courage, for there would be nothing to fear. If evil did not exist, man could only love his friends; he could never learn to love even his enemies. Without evil, there would be no enemies.[28] Only an infinite God can know all the good He will bring out of evil (Isaiah 55:8-9).

Fourth, Geisler and Corduan argue that an all-good and all-powerful God is not required to create the best possible world. They reason that all He can be expected to do is create the best possible way to achieve the greatest possible world. Heaven is the greatest possible world.[29]

Several other points could also be made. First, the atheist usually denies the existence of objective evil since he knows that this would admit to the existence of the absolute moral law.[30] The atheist knows that once he acknowledges the absolute moral law, the existence of God (the absolute moral law Giver) surely will follow.[31] For evil to be objectively real, it must exist as a perversion of that which is ultimately good. To escape this conclusion, the atheist usually chooses to deny the existence of evil. Therefore, it is rather ironic that the atheist (who usually denies the existence of evil) attempts to use evil to disprove the existence of the God of the Bible. The presence of evil may be problematic for all other world views (including Christian theism), but it is totally devastating to atheism. If there is no God, then there are also no objective moral values. The most consistent atheists, such as Nietzsche, have readily admitted this.[32]

Second, all world views must deal with the problem of evil, but the God of the Bible is the only guarantee that evil will ultimately be defeated.[33] The God of deism is no longer concerned with the problems of this world (such as evil).[34] In pantheism, evil is an illusion.[35] In atheism, there is no basis to call anything evil.[36] But, the biblical God guarantees that evil will be defeated through Christ's death, resurrection, and return (John 1:29; 1 Peter 2:24; 3:18; Romans 4:25; Isaiah 9:6-7; 11:1-9; Zechariah 9:9-10; Revelation 20;4-6).

Third, non-Christians act as if the existence of evil is an unexpected factor in the Christian world view, but this is not the case. God would not have given mankind the Bible had it not been for the problem of evil. If man had not fallen into sin in the garden, he would have had no need for salvation (Genesis 3:1-7; Romans

3:10, 23; 5:12; 6:23). The Bible could actually be titled "God's Solution to the Problem of Evil."

In short, the solution to the moral problem of evil (how an all-good, all-powerful God can co-exist with evil) is that God gave humans and angels free will. It is the abuse of this free will by humans and angels that has brought evil and human suffering into existence. God created the possibility for evil (by giving man and angels free will), not evil itself.

Christian philosopher Alvin Plantinga adds an important detail concerning the Christian response to the moral problem of evil. He writes that there are two ways Christians can respond to this dilemma. First, he may develop a free will theodicy. A theodicy is an attempt to explain what was God's reason (or reasons) for allowing evil. On the other hand, according to Plantinga, the Christian does not have to go that far. Instead of presenting a free will theodicy, he may develop a free will defense. In this case, rather than attempting to explain the reason as to why God allows evil and human suffering, the Christian can merely suggest a *possible* reason why God has allowed evil and human suffering.[37] The free will defense, according to Plantinga, is sufficient in itself to show that the existence of evil does not rule out the possible existence of the God of theism.[38]

In other words, since the problem of evil is an attempt to prove God's existence as being impossible, the Christian only needs to provide possible solutions to this problem. Once this is done, God's existence will have been shown to be possible. Further argumentation (such as the cosmological, teleological, moral, and ontological arguments) can then be presented to argue for God's existence with a higher degree of probability.[39]

THE PHYSICAL PROBLEM OF EVIL

The physical or natural problem of evil deals with evil not directly connected to the abuse of human freedom.[40] All physical or natural evil is at least indirectly related to the abuse of human freedom. Without the Fall of man in history, creation would still be perfect (Genesis 1:31). Still, much physical evil is not directly related to human choices. Natural disasters such as earthquakes, floods, hurricanes, and deaths of innocent infants are examples of physical evil.

Geisler and Corduan list five explanations for physical evil.[41] None of the five are meant to be all-encompassing. Each explains some of the physical evil that occurs. First, some physical evil is necessary for moral perfection.[42] There can be no courage without something evil to fear. Misery is needed for there to be sympathy. Tribulation is needed for there to be endurance and patience.[43] For God to build these characteristics in man, He must permit a certain amount of physical evil.

Second, human free choices do cause some physical evil.[44] It would be an obvious error to assume that no physical evil is caused by the abuse of human free will. The choice to drink and drive has caused much physical evil. Many infants have been born with an addiction to cocaine due to their mothers' choice to abuse drugs while pregnant. It is impossible for God to remove all physical evil without tampering with human free will.[45] It is even possible that some major natural disasters are caused by the evil choices of humans. According to the Bible, this was the case with Sodom and Gomorrah (Genesis 18:20-21; 19).

Third, some physical evil is caused by the choices of demons.[46] The Scriptures speak of demons (fallen angels led by Satan) causing suffering to humans (Job 1, 2; Mark 5:1-20). Demons oppose God and His plans, but they will ultimately be defeated by Christ (Revelation 19, 20, 21, 22).

Fourth, God often uses physical evil as a moral warning.[47] Physical pain is often a warning that greater suffering will follow if behavior is not changed. Examples of this would be excessive coughing that is often caused by smoking and heavy breathing caused by over training during a physical workout. Also, God may use pain and suffering to cause a person to focus on Him, rather than on worldly pleasures.[48]

Fifth, some physical evils are necessary in the present state of the physical world.[49] To survive, animals often eat other animals. Humans eat animals as well. It appears that, at least in the present state of the creation, lower life forms are subjected to pain and death in order to facilitate the preservation of higher life forms.[50]

Physical evil, therefore, does not present insurmountable problems for Christian theism. Though man is limited in knowledge and cannot infallibly ascertain why God allows each and every case of physical evil, the five reasons given above should suffice to show that the presence of physical evil in no way rules out the existence of the God of the Bible.

CONCLUSION

Once the Christian apologist has provided strong evidence for God's existence, he need only give possible reasons why an all-good and all-powerful God would allow evil and human suffering. God has good reasons for allowing evil and human suffering, even though we may not know them fully. Therefore, the existence of evil does not disprove the existence of an all-good and all-powerful God. These two are not mutually exclusive.

ENDNOTES

1. Ronald Nash, *Faith and Reason* (Grand Rapids: Zondervan Publishing House, 1988), 177.
2. Geisler and Corduan, *Philosophy of Religion* (Grand Rapids: Baker Book House, 1988), 318.
3. Ibid.
4. Ibid., 333.
5. Ibid.
6. Ibid., 364.
7. Ibid.
8. Ibid.
9. Nash, 179-180.
10. Ibid.
11. Ibid., 180.
12. Geisler and Corduan, 318.
13. Mary Baker Eddy, *Science and Health with Key to the Scriptures* (Boston: The First Church of Christ, Scientist, 1971), 293, 447, 472, 480, 482.
14. Geisler and Corduan, 318-319.
15. Ibid., 319.
16. Ibid., 319-320.
17. Ibid., 318-320.
18. Augustine, *City of God*, 11.9, 12.3, 14.11, 22.1.
19. Geisler and Corduan, 323-324.
20. Thomas Aquinas, *Summa Theologiae: A Concise Translation*, edited by Timothy McDermott (Westminster, MD: Christian Classics, 1989), 91-92.
21. Geisler and Corduan, 320-330.
22. Ibid., 333.
23. Harold S. Kushner, *When Bad Things Happen to Good People* (New York: Avon Books, 1981), 129,134,145-148.
24. Geisler and Corduan, 334.
25. Ibid., 348.
26. Ibid.
27. Ibid.

28. Ibid.

29. Ibid., 342-343.

30. C. S. Lewis, *Mere Christianity* (New York: MacMillian Publishing Company, 1952), 34-39.

31. Ibid.

32. Friedrich Nietzsche, *The Portable Nietzsche*, ed. by Walter Kaufmann, (New York: Penguin Books, 1982), 228.

33. Geisler and Watkins, *Worlds Apart* (Grand Rapids: Baker Book House, 1989), 41.

34. Ibid., 148-149.

35. Ibid., 99-100.

36. Ibid., 59.

37. Alvin Plantinga, *God, Freedom, and Evil* (Grand Rapids: William B. Eerdmans Publishing Company, 1974), 28.

38. Ibid.

39. Ibid.

40. Geisler and Corduan, 364.

41. Ibid., 372-378.

42. Ibid., 372-373.

43. Ibid., 372.

44. Ibid., 373.

45. Ibid., 373-374.

46. Ibid., 375.

47. Ibid., 376.

48. Ibid.

49. Ibid.

50. Ibid., 376-378.

Chapter Seven

Are Moral Absolutes Real?

Ethics deals with issues of morality, that which is right and wrong.[1] The Christian ethical perspective holds to absolute moral values, laws that are universally binding. Often, non-Christian views hold to moral relativism. Consistent atheists are moral relativists-since they deny the existence of God (the absolute moral Lawgiver), they deny the existence of absolute moral laws. Moral relativism rejects the idea that there are objective, universal rights and wrongs.[2] What is right for one person is not necessarily right for another person, and vice versa. Each person decides what is right for himself. Many atheists and pantheists are moral relativists.[3]

The new atheists are inconsistent on this point. Often, they imply that there are no moral absolutes (a view which is consistent with their atheism). But, at other times, they act as if they believe in moral absolutes in order to condemn Christianity or the God of the Bible. The new atheists also try to create an ethic of compassion based on atheistic evolution. I believe they fail miserably in this area. If there is no God, what place is left for compassion?

Atheists of the past tended to be more consistent with their atheism; they tended to be moral relativists. We will now discuss some of the relativistic views of atheists of the past, and then offer a refutation of moral relativism.

AN EXAMINATION OF MORAL RELATIVISM

Friedrich Nietzsche (1844-1900) was a German philosopher. He believed that the advances of human knowledge had proven that belief in God was a mere superstition. Nietzsche therefore reasoned that since "God is dead," all traditional values have died with Him. Nietzsche was angered with his atheistic colleagues who were unwilling to dismiss traditional moral absolutes which had no justification without God's existence.[4]

Nietzsche preached that a group of "supermen" must arise with the courage to create their own values through their "will to power." Nietzsche rejected the "soft" values of Christianity (brotherly love, turning the other cheek, charity, compassion, etc.); he felt they hindered man's creativity and potential. He recommended that the supermen create their own "hard" values that would allow man to realize his creative potential.[5] Nietzsche was very consistent with his atheism. He realized that without God, there are no universal moral values. Man is free to create his own values. It is interesting to note that the Nazis often referred to Nietzsche's writings for the supposed intellectual justification for their acts of cruelty.[6]

Many other atheists agree with Nietzsche concerning moral relativism. British philosopher Bertrand Russell (1872-1970) once wrote, "Outside human desires there is no moral standard."[7] A. J. Ayer believed that moral commands did not result from any objective standard above man. Instead, Ayer stated that moral commands merely express one's subjective feelings. When one says that murder is wrong, one is merely saying that he feels that murder is wrong.[8] Jean-Paul Sartre, a French existentialist, believed that there is no objective meaning to life. Therefore, according to Sartre, man must create his own values.[9]

There are many different ways that moral relativists attempt to determine what action should be taken. Hedonism is probably the most extreme. It declares that whatever brings the most pleasure is right. In other words, if it feels good, do it.[10] If this position is true, then there is no basis from which to judge the actions of Adolph Hitler as being evil.[11]

Utilitarianism teaches that man should attempt to bring about the greatest good for the greatest number of people.[12] Utilitarianism is problematic. First, "good" is a meaningless term if moral relativism is true, for then there would be no such thing as good or evil. Second, to say that man "should" do something is to introduce a universal moral command. However, there is no room for universal moral commands in moral relativism.[13]

Joseph Fletcher founded "situation ethics." Situation ethics is the view that ethics are relative to the situation. Fletcher claimed that he was not a moral relativist. He believed that there was only one moral absolute: love. Still, his concept of love was so void of meaning that his view of ethics, for all practical purposes, is synonymous with moral relativism.[14]

Now, the new atheists have arrived on the intellectual scene. They speak as if atheistic evolution can produce universal moral laws. They often borrow moral laws from the Christian world view while, at the same time, rejecting the Christian world view. They are not consistent with their atheism. Human rights, rights for minorities, and loving one's neighbor make sense in the Christian world view. But, these moral views do not make sense in an atheist world. If we were to derive moral laws from atheistic, Darwinian evolution, these evolutionary moral laws would entail the "survival of the fittest" mentality. Social Darwinists of the early twentieth century show this to be the case by their promoting the eugenics movement—the idea that only the mentally and physically healthy humans should be allowed to reproduce. In short, if there is an atheist absolute moral law produced by evolutionary processes, it would be the ethic of Hitler or Stalin, not the ethic of Jesus or Mother Theresa. On the other hand, if there is an atheist moral absolute law, since it evolved into existence and is still evolving, it is not really "absolute;" it is not eternal and unchanging. If evolution is true, everything is in a state of flux. And, that would include moral laws. Hence, though the new atheists regularly make moral pronouncements, in the end, they themselves are moral relativists.

REFUTING MORAL RELATIVISM

In response to Joseph Fletcher, the situation never determines what is right. It is God who determines what is right. Still, the situation may aid the Christian in finding which of God's laws should be applied.[15] For, when two of God's commands come in conflict due to a situation so that a person cannot obey both, God requires that the person obey the greater command. God then exempts the person from obeying the lesser command. An example of this is the fact that God compliments Rahab the Harlot for lying in order to save two innocent lives (Joshua 2; Hebrews 11:31; James 2:25).[16]

Moral relativists deny the absolute moral law. Still, they, like all people, recognize the evil actions of others when they are wronged. When they are wronged, they appeal to an objective and universal law that stands above man. Moral relativists deny absolute moral law in the lecture hall, but they live by it in their everyday lives.[17] Moral relativists reserve the right for themselves to call the actions of Hitler wrong,[18] but if there is no such thing as right and wrong (as the moral relativists say), they cannot really call any action wrong. The moral law does not ultimately come from within each individual, for then no one could call the actions of another evil.[19]

The moral law does not ultimately come from each society, for then one society could not call the actions of another society (such as Nazi Germany) wrong.[20] Finally, the moral law does not ultimately come from world consensus,[21] for world consensus is often wrong. World consensus once thought the world was flat. World consensus once considered slavery morally permissible.

Appealing to world or societal consensus as the ultimate source of the moral law is actually just an extension of the view that the individual is the ultimate source. The difference is only quantitative (the number of people increases). However, for there to be a moral law above all men (in order to judge all men), this moral law must be qualitatively above all men (not just quantitatively greater than the few). If there is an absolute moral law qualitatively above all men, all societies, and the world consensus, then there must be an absolute moral law Giver that stands qualitatively above all men, all societies, and world consensus.

The absolute moral law is eternal and unchanging. We use it to condemn the actions of past generations. Since the moral law is eternal and unchanging, the moral law Giver must also be eternal and unchanging. The moral law is not descriptive of what is; it is prescriptive of what should be.[22] Prescriptive laws need a Prescriber.

Since the absolute moral law leads directly to the existence of the theistic God (the absolute moral law Giver), many atheists and pantheists may feel compelled to reject its existence. Also, people who wish to live promiscuous lives often choose to reject God's existence. The apostle John appears to be talking about these people when he says:

And this is the judgment, that the light is come into the world, and men loved the darkness rather than the light; for their deeds were evil. For everyone who does evil hates the light, and does not come to the light, lest his deeds should be exposed (John 3:19-20).

Can Atheists Be Moral?

Two other issues dealing with morality need to be mentioned. First, the new atheists claim that atheists can be moral—they are often as moral as Christians. However, from the Christian perspective, we are all sinners. We all stand condemned before a holy God. We can only please God by coming to Him through faith in Jesus His Son. None of us are good in God's eyes in our own strength (John 15:5). Still, atheists can be good in the eyes of other men—they can be good neighbors. They can be good citizens. No Christian should deny this. Because we were created in God's image, God has placed His moral laws within our hearts and in our consciences (Romans 2:14-15). Therefore, deep down inside, even atheists know right from wrong, and they sometimes choose to do the right thing. Even though no one can save himself by his works, atheists can be moral and law-abiding in the eyes of other men. The fact that atheists can be moral in this sense in no way detracts from God being the source of absolute moral laws.

Did Morality Evolve Into Existence?

Second, since the new atheists believe that everything can be explained through atheistic evolution, they believe that moral laws evolved into existence. However, if this is the case, this morality would not be an ethic of compassion, but a survival of the fittest ethic. Social Darwinists of the early twentieth century understood this. They promoted eugenics—the idea that weaker members of the human race should not be allowed to reproduce. (In fact, even Darwin admitted this in his work *The Descent of Man.*) Today, evolutionary ethics promote abortion, euthanasia, and infanticide. Evolutionary ethics is the ethics of the Third Reich; it is a Master Race ideology. For example, Darwinian ethicist Peter Singer of Princeton believes that not all human life is worth living and that we should euthanize those whose quality of life does not meet our standard. Though the new atheists are not explicitly calling for a Nazi ethic, the logical outcome of their views, if widely accepted, will produce a brave new world of genocide. Without the God of the Bible, the moral foundations of civilization will crumble. If God is dead, man is dead as well. Without God, human life is not sacred. In a universe without God, there are no human rights.

ENDNOTES

1. Geisler and Feinberg, *Introduction to Philosophy* (Grand Rapids: Baker Book House, 1980), 24-26.
2. Moreland, *Scaling the Secular City*, (Grand Rapids: Baker Book House, 1987), 240.
3. Geisler and Watkins, *Worlds Apart* (Grand Rapids: Baker Book House, 1989). 59, 99-100.
4. Friedrich Nietzsche, *The Portable Nietzsche*, ed. by Walter Kaufmann (New York: Penguin Books, 1982), 95-96, 143, 228.
5. Ibid., 124-125, 139, 191, 197-198.
6. Frederick Copleston, *A History of Philosophy* (New York: Doubleday, 1960), vol. 7, 403.
7. Bertrand Russell, *Why I am not a Christian* (New York: Simon and Schuster, 1957), 62.
8. Norman L. Geisler, *Christian Ethics* (Grand Rapids: Baker Book House, 1989), 32.
9. Geisler and Feinberg, 406.
10. Ibid., 400-401.
11. Geisler, *Christian Ethics*, 36-37.
12. Ibid., 63.
13. Ibid., 73-75.
14. Ibid., 43-61.
15. Geisler and Feinberg, 411.
16. Ibid., 424-427.
17. Hodge, *Systematic Theology*. (Grand Rapids: Eerdmans Publishing Company, 1989), vol. 1, 210.
18. Hick, *The Existence of God*, (New York: The MacMillian Company, 1964), 183-186.
19. Moreland, 246-247.
20. Ibid., 243-244.
21. Geisler and Feinberg, 355.
22. C. S. Lewis, *Mere Christianity*, (New York: The MacMillian Company, 1952), 27-28.

Chapter Eight

Are Miracles Possible?

Richard Dawkins, Christopher Hitchens, and their new atheist buddies believe that belief in miracles is pre-scientific superstition, and that no rational person would accept the possibility of a miracle actually occurring. They act as if before Charles Darwin came along mankind didn't know that a virgin birth or a bodily resurrection could not be explained through natural laws. Even the ancients understood that virgins do not normally give birth to babies and that dead people stay dead. That's why the ancients believed the virgin birth and bodily resurrection of Jesus were miracles—because the laws of nature were superseded. The new atheists are biased against the possibility of miracles. They begin their assessment of Christianity by assuming (without proof) that miracles are impossible, and then reject the Gospel accounts because of its miracle claims.

Christianity is a religion based in history. The claims, death, and resurrection of Jesus of Nazareth occurred in history. For this reason, historical evidence is of great importance. If one can prove that Jesus really did rise from the dead in history, then one will have gone a long way towards establishing Christianity as the true religion. However, before an apologist can engage in presenting historical evidences for the resurrection of Christ, he must first answer the philosophical objections against the possibility of miracles. If miracles are by definition impossible, then it makes no sense to look into history to see if Jesus really rose from the dead.

The strongest philosophical argumentation against miracles came from the pens of Benedict Spinoza (1632-1677) and David Hume (1711-1776). Spinoza was a pantheist.[1] He believed in an impersonal god that was identical to the universe. He reasoned that an impersonal god could not choose to perform miracles, for only personal beings make choices. Whatever an impersonal god does, it must do by necessity. Spinoza believed that nature necessarily operates in a uniform manner. Therefore, he argued that the laws of nature cannot be violated. Since miracles would be violations of the laws of nature, they are impossible.[2]

David Hume was a deist. He believed that after God created the universe, He no longer involved Himself with His creation. Hume reasoned that miracles, if they occur, are very rare events. On the other hand, the laws of nature describe repeatable, everyday occurrences. Hume argued that the wise man will always base his beliefs on the highest degree of probability. Since the laws of nature have a high degree of probability while a miracle is improbable, Hume considered the evidence against miracles always greater than the evidence for miracles. Therefore, according to Hume, the wise man will always reject the proposed miracle.[3]

RESPONSE TO SPINOZA

Spinoza argued that miracles are impossible. Several things should be mentioned in refutation of Spinoza's argument. Though it is true that a pantheistic god cannot choose to perform a miracle (a pantheistic god is impersonal and, therefore, cannot choose anything), there is strong evidence that a pantheistic god does not exist.[4] As the cosmological argument has shown, a theistic God exists.[5] A theistic God is a personal God, and a personal God *can* choose to perform miracles.

Second, Spinoza's premise that the laws of nature can never be violated is suspect. The laws of nature are descriptive; they are not prescriptive. In other words, the laws of nature describe the way nature usually acts. The laws of nature do not prescribe how nature must act.[6]

Third, Spinoza's definition of a miracle as a violation of the laws of nature is objectionable. It is possible that miracles do not violate the laws of nature; they merely supersede the laws of nature. C. S. Lewis argued along these lines.[7]

Fourth, if God created the universe, then the laws of nature are subject to Him. God can choose to suspend or violate (depending on how one defines a miracle) the laws of nature any time He wishes. In short, Spinoza has failed to show that miracles are impossible.

RESPONSE TO HUME

Hume, unlike Spinoza, did not argue for the impossibility of miracles. Instead, he argued that miracles were so unlikely that the evidence against them will always be greater than the evidence for them. Hume argued that miracles are improbable, and that the wise man will only believe that which is probable. Hence, the wise man will never accept evidence for a miracle.[8]

The Christian apologist can respond to Hume's reasoning in the following manner. Just because usual events (the laws of nature) occur more often does not mean that the wise man will never believe that an unusual event (a miracle) has occurred.[9] The wise man should not *a priori* rule out the possibility of miracles. The wise man will examine the evidence for or against a miracle claim, and base his judgment on the evidence. Since there were over 500 witnesses who claimed to have seen Jesus risen from the dead (1 Corinthians 15:3-8), a wise man would not reject the miracle of the resurrection merely because all other men have remained dead. It seems that a wise man would examine a miracle claim if there are reliable eyewitnesses. If there is no good reason to reject the testimony of reliable eyewitnesses, it seems that a wise man would accept their testimony that a miracle has occurred.

CONTEMPORARY WESTERN ACADEMIC BIAS AGAINST MIRACLES

Contemporary anthropological studies have shown that the non-Western world does not agree with the Western academic bias against miracles. In fact, many current anthropologists accuse Western scholars who are biased against miracles of ethnocentrism—believing their culture is superior to other cultures.[10]

Also, even Westerners in general do not agree with the Western academic bias against miracles. Recent surveys show that over 80% of Americans still believe that miracles are possible.[11] So, outside of the Western academic establishment, most people are willing to examine evidence for or against miracles—they are open to the possibility of miracles. It appears that Western scholars who have a bias against miracles are not only out of touch with the non-Western world, but they are apparently out of touch with most Westerners as well. The Western academic bias against miracles is not justified. Miracle claims should be investigated, rather than ruled out in a biased, a priori manner.

CONCLUSION

Some people will not accept any event unless it has a natural cause. Therefore, they reject miracles because they have a supernatural Cause (God).[12] But, the cosmological argument has shown that the universe itself needs a supernatural Cause (God). Therefore, if there is a God who created the universe, then He would have no problem intervening in His universe by supernaturally working miracles within it. A person cannot rule out miracles simply because his world view does not allow them. If his world view is weak (such as pantheism and deism), then he has weak reasons for rejecting miracles. If, on the other hand, a person has strong evidence for his world view (such as theism), and that world view is consistent with the reality of miracles, then that person has strong reasons for believing that miracles are possible.

This chapter has only shown that miracles are possible. Historical evidence must be examined to see whether miracles have actually occurred. Philosophical argumentation can only show that miracles are possible. Historical evidences must be utilized to determine if an alleged miracle (such as the resurrection of Jesus from the dead) has in fact occurred.

ENDNOTES

1. Norman L. Geisler, *Miracles and the Modern Mind* (Grand Rapids: Baker Book House, 1992), 18.
2. Ibid., 15.
3. David Hume, *An Inquiry Concerning Human Understanding* (New York: The Liberal Arts Press, 1955), 117-141.
4. A pantheistic God cannot explain the existence of evil, absolute moral laws, personality, the beginning of the universe, meaning in life, etc.
5. See Chapters 3 and 4 of this book.
6. Terry L. Miethe, ed. *Did Jesus Rise From the Dead?* (San Francisco: Harper and Row, 1987), 18.
7. C. S. Lewis, *Miracles* (New York: Collier Books, 1960), 59-60.
8. Geisler, 23-28.
9. Ibid., 27-31.
10. Gregory Boyd and Paul Eddy, *The Jesus Legend* (Grand Rapids: Baker Book House, 2007), 67-90.
11. Ibid.
12. Ibid., 50-51.

Chapter Nine

What Do Christians Believe?

What do Christians believe? There are nine doctrines that traditional, Bible-believing Christians acknowledge: 1) the doctrine of the Trinity, 2) creation by God, 3) biblical inspiration and inerrancy, 4) salvation by God's grace alone through faith alone in Jesus alone, 5) the virgin birth of Jesus, 6) the deity of Christ, 7) the bodily resurrection of Jesus, 8) the visible return of Jesus, and 9) the substitutionary death of Christ. This chapter will explain what traditional Christians believe. We have already defended the existence of God. In the remainder of this book, we will only be able to defend the reliability of the New Testament, Jesus' deity, and His resurrection. Once we acknowledge Jesus' deity, then His teachings take on absolute authority. From Jesus' teachings we can derive the validity of the rest of the Christian beliefs listed above.

THE DOCTRINE OF THE TRINITY

First, *the doctrine of the Trinity* is the Christian belief that there is only one God, but this one true God is three co-equal, co-eternal Persons. The Bible clearly teaches that there is only one God (Isaiah 43:10; 44:6; 46:9; 1 Timothy 2:5). The Father is referred to as God (Galatians 1:1; 1 Peter 1:1). However, the Son (Jesus) and the Holy Spirit are also called God (John 1:1; 5:18;

10:30-33; Titus 2:13; 2 Peter 1:1; Acts 5:3-4; 1 Corinthians 3:16). Because of these passages, some students of the Bible assume that the Father, Son, and Holy Spirit are the same person. However, this is opposed to what the scriptures teach, for the Bible affirms that the Father, Son, and Holy Spirit are three separate persons (Matthew 3:16-17; John 14:16-17, 26; 15:26). When all this biblical data is gathered, the doctrine of the Trinity becomes evident. This doctrine teaches that there is only one true God, and that this one true God eternally exists as three equal Persons (the Father, Son, and Holy Spirit).

Though this doctrine is not self-contradictory, it is above human understanding as to how one being (God) could be three Persons. Still, an illustration may be helpful. A single-celled animal has one cell and is one being. Though a man is also only one being, he has trillions of cells that comprise his body. If a single-celled animal had understanding, it would probably have difficulty believing that one being (a man) could be more than one cell. This is analogous to man's relationship to God. Since man is only one being and only one person, it transcends his limited understanding as to how God could be only one Being, yet three Persons.

Still, the Bible teaches this doctrine, and, as will be shown later, there are good reasons for believing the Bible is God's inerrant word. Therefore, though it is above human reason, defenders of the faith should humbly accept the doctrine of the Trinity. It is only reasonable that certain aspects of God's nature go beyond human reason. For the unlimited Creator's existence transcends the limited existence of His creatures.

CREATION BY GOD

Second, traditional Christians believe that *God created the universe and man*. Though theistic evolutionists can be saved and often are, evolution was proposed by scientists in an attempt to explain away any need for God's existence. If it can be shown that God exists, evolution becomes an unnecessary belief system. Also, the supposed evidence for evolution is very unconvincing (as was shown in chapter three). In reality, evolution is only one way to interpret the evidence; it is not what the evidence demands.

If a Christian accepts evolution, then many problems arise. For the Bible declares that God formed Adam from the ground (Genesis 2:7). Adam did not, according to the Bible, evolve from apes. Nor did his wife Eve, for the scriptures declare that God formed her from Adam's side (Genesis 2:21-22). Since all mankind came from this couple, there is no room for a theistic-evolutionary interpretation of man's origin. Once must choose between the biblical account of creation or atheistic evolution. They are mutually-exclusive.

Scriptures declare death to be a consequence of the fall (Genesis 2:16-17; Romans 5:12; 6:23), for all that God created was good (Genesis 1:31). The creation was not cursed until after the Fall of man (Genesis 3:17-19; Romans 8:18-22). But, if evolution is true, there would be death and suffering before the Fall of man. This appears inconsistent with the concept of a perfect creation before the Fall. Though Christians may disagree as to whether the earth is old or young, to accept evolution would be to contradict the Bible's account of both creation and the Fall. Therefore, the Christian should reject evolution entirely.

BIBLICAL INSPIRATION AND INERRANCY

The third belief is the doctrine of *biblical inspiration and inerrancy*. The Bible clearly teaches that it itself is the Word of God (2 Timothy 3:16-17). All that God says is true (Proverbs 30:5-6; John 17:17). God guided human authors to record His word without errors. The apostle Peter made it clear that the Bible is not a book that records the mere speculation of men. He stated that, "no prophecy was ever made by an act of human will, but men moved by the Holy Spirit spoke from God" (2 Peter 1:20-21). Jesus taught that not only are the ideas of the Bible inspired, but so are the words themselves (Matthew 5:18). For the Christian to take any lesser view of Scripture would greatly compromise his faithfulness to the Lord.

SALVATION BY GOD'S GRACE THROUGH FAITH IN CHRIST ALONE

Fourth, the traditional Christian accepts the doctrine of *salvation by God's grace alone through faith alone in Christ alone*. The Bible teaches that salvation cannot be earned. For all men are sinners who cannot save themselves (Romans 3:10, 23; Matthew 19:25-26). We inherited a sin nature from Adam who fell into sin in the Garden of Eden (Romans 5:12; Genesis 3:1-7). Jesus is the only way for man to be saved (John 14:6; Acts 4:12). A person must put his trust in Jesus as Savior if he is to escape the eternal flames of hell (John 3:16-18; 11:25-26; Ephesians 2:8-9; Revelation 20:15). It must also be noted that a person cannot accept God the Father if he rejects God the Son (1 John 2:23; Luke 10:16). There is no such thing as a person who believes in the true God but rejects the true Savior. God sent His Son as the only way for us to be saved. Though a Christian is not saved by good works, true saving faith will produce good works in his life (James 2:26; Romans 3:31). This doctrine of salvation by God's grace through faith in Christ alone is essential. One cannot be a true believer if the biblical view of salvation is denied (Galatians 1:8-9).

THE VIRGIN BIRTH OF CHRIST

Fifth, the Christian believes in *the virgin birth of Christ.* Though this is not essential to salvation, those who reject this doctrine usually reject other teachings which are essential (such as the deity of Christ). The Bible teaches that Jesus had no human father. He was born of the Virgin Mary through the miraculous work of the Holy Spirit (Isaiah 7:14; Matthew 1:18-25; Luke 1:35). If God managed to create the universe out of nothing, He would have no problem making a baby without the agency of a man. If Jesus had two human parents, His claim to be God would seem questionable, for how would He be different from any other man since each had two parents as well? But if Jesus had one human parent, He would still be fully human (for His human nature would have been inherited from his human parent). And if God was His Father, Jesus could be fully God (He would share the divine nature of His Father). When one denies the virgin birth, the deity of Christ usually falls as well.

THE DEITY OF CHRIST

Sixth, Christians accept *the deity of Christ.* This doctrine is essential for salvation. A person cannot be saved while rejecting Christ's deity (John 8:23-24). There are many Bible passages which teach that Jesus is God. The Old Testament prophets teach that the Jewish Messiah is God (Isaiah 7:14; 9:6; Jeremiah 23:5-6; Zechariah 14:5; Micah 5:2), and the New Testament confirms that Jesus is the Jewish Messiah (Mark 14:61-62; John 4:25-26). The apostles Matthew, John, Thomas, Peter, and Paul clearly referred to Jesus as God (Matthew 1:23; John 1:1, 14; 20:26-29; 2 Peter 1:1; Philippians 2:5-6; Colossians 2:9; Titus 2:13). Even God the Father called Jesus God (Hebrews 1:8).

117

On numerous occasions, Jesus claimed to be God (John 5:17-18; 8:23-24, 58-59; 10:28-33; 14:9). He accepted worship (Matthew 2:11; 28:9, 17; John 9:35-38) and expected the same honor for Himself that was due God the Father (John 5:22-23). He claimed to have shared the Father's glory with Him before the world was created (John 17:5). Jesus forgave sins (Mark 2:5-12) and was crucified for claiming to be God (Mark 14: 61-64). No true Christian can deny that Jesus is God.

THE BODILY RESURRECTION OF CHRIST

Seventh, the Christian believes in *the bodily resurrection of Christ*. Paul states that a person must believe that Jesus rose from the dead if he is to be saved (Romans 10:9). Paul included Christ's resurrection as an essential component of the gospel he preached (1 Corinthians 15:1-4). Though many cultists deny that Christ rose bodily from the dead, the Jewish concept of resurrection always entailed the raising of the same body that had previously died. Since the Christian concept of resurrection was derived from Jewish thought, this argues strongly for Christ's bodily resurrection.

New Testament evidence for Christ's bodily resurrection is abundant. Jesus appeared numerous times to witnesses after His death and resurrection (1 Corinthians 15:3-8). Jesus gave these witnesses convincing evidences that He had risen in the same body in which He had died (John 20:24-29; Luke 24:36-43). In fact, at an earlier time, He had predicted He would raise His own body from the dead (John 2:19-21).

Though He was raised in the same body in which He had died, this body was glorified and received powers it had not previously possessed (1 Corinthians 15:35-54). The apostle Paul stressed the importance of the resurrection by declaring that if Jesus had not risen from the dead, then faith in Him and preaching the gospel is worthless. If Jesus did not rise, then Christians will die in their sins (1 Corinthians 15:14, 17).

THE BODILY AND VISIBLE RETURN OF CHRIST

Eighth, true Christians accept *the bodily and visible return of Christ*. The Bible is very clear that Jesus will someday return to the planet earth (Matthew 24:29-31; John 14:2-3). Christ's return will be visible (Revelation 1:7) and bodily (Acts 1:10-11; Zechariah 12:10). Jesus will return to gather believers (John 14:1-3; 1 Thessalonians 4:13-18) and to judge nonbelievers (Revelation 19:11-21; 2 Thessalonians 1:6-10). Jesus will bring the Kingdom of God to earth (Revelation 11:15).

The bodily and visible return of Christ to earth is important for two reasons. First, it is the blessed hope of the church (Titus 2:13). Christians must continue to remind themselves that our hope is not founded in the things of this world. Second, Peter predicted that in the last days mockers would come denying Christ's return (2 Peter 3:3-4). These mockers must be confronted; their false teachings must be refuted.

THE SUBSTITUTIONARY DEATH OF CHRIST

Ninth, the Christian accepts *the substitutionary death of Christ*. This is an essential Christian belief. To deny it is to deny the faith. Jesus did not die on the cross to merely set an example for others or to encourage others to live moral lives. The significance of His death goes far beyond this. Jesus died on the cross for the sins of mankind (Matthew 1:21; John 1:29; 2 Corinthians 5:21). He took the punishment that man deserves (1 Peter 2:24; 3:18). Since God is totally just, He can only forgive sin

119

if it has been paid for in full. Jesus, through His death on the cross, paid the price for the sins of mankind (Mark 10:45; 2 Peter 2:1). He took the penalty man deserves; He substituted Himself for man. Because of Jesus, those who put their faith in Him are no longer under the judgment of God (1 Corinthians 5:7).

WE MUST HAVE GENUINE LOVE FOR THE NEW ATHEISTS

Finally, it goes without saying that true believers should have genuine love for both the saved and the unsaved. We must love the new atheists-ultimately, they are not our real enemies-Satan and his demons are (Ephesians 6:10-12). Jesus commands His followers to love their neighbors as themselves (Mark 12:31). He also commands Christians to love their enemies (Matthew 5:43-48). The apostle Paul commands believers to speak the truth in love (Ephesians 4:15).

God desires all men to be saved (2 Peter 3:9; 1 Timothy 2:1-6). God loves all mankind (John 3:16; Romans 5:8). Therefore, Christians should also love all men and seek their salvation. Jesus has died for all mankind (1 John 2:2; 2 Corinthians 5:15). Therefore, it is the responsibility of the church to share the gospel message with all mankind (Matthew 28:19-20) and to defend the faith once for all delivered to the saints (1 Peter 3:15; Jude 3). Still, love must be the primary motivation. Without a genuine love for people, one should not engage in evangelism or the defense of the faith. The apostle Paul said it best:

If I speak with the tongues of men and of angels, but do not have love, I have become a noisy gong or a clanging cymbal. And if I have the gift of prophecy, and know all mysteries and all knowledge; and if I have all faith, so as to remove mountains, but do not have love, I am nothing. And if I give all my possessions to feed the poor, and if I deliver my body to be burned, but do not have love, it profits me nothing (1 Corinthians 13:1-3).

Chapter Ten

Is the New Testament Historically Reliable?

Evidence the New Testament is Reliable

Christopher Hitchens and Richard Dawkins (as well as the rest of the new atheists) simply do not take Christianity seriously. They consider "religious faith" to be superstitious and antiquated. They do not believe educated, intelligent people should entertain religious beliefs. In short, Hitchens and Dawkins never disprove Christianity—they merely assume that science and philosophy have disproven it. They assume miracles are impossible so the miracle claims of Christianity must be false. However, we have shown that the bias against the possibility of miracles is a weak, philosophical bias that assumes what is supposed to be proved. Miracles are possible; hence, we must take Christianity's truth claims seriously and examine the evidence for or against Christianity.

In the next three chapters, we will make a case for the historical reliability of the New Testament manuscripts and then argue that the Jesus of the Bible is the true Jesus of history. In short, Jesus claimed to be God incarnate, the Jewish Messiah, and the Savior of the world, and then He bodily rose from the dead to prove those claims true.

First, *there is strong evidence that the New Testament is historically reliable*. There is more manuscript evidence and external evidence for the reliability of the New Testament documents than for any other writing of the first century ad. Most ancient documents have few surviving copies, yet historians are confident of their reliability. But, the New Testament has by far the greatest manuscript evidence for its reliability when compared with other first-century writings.

The New Testament was written in Koine or common Greek. There are over 5,700 hand-written Greek manuscripts of the New Testament still in existence today. Also, we have over 9,000 New Testament manuscripts in other ancient languages (i.e., Syriac, Coptic, Latin, Arabic). In fact, the entire New Testament, except for eleven verses, can be reproduced from the writings of the church fathers of the second and third centuries.[1] No other first-century ad writing comes close to the New Testament in manuscript support. It is by far the most reliable of all ancient documents. If historians do not reject other first century writings, they should not question the reliability of the New Testament.

Some of the earliest portions of the New Testament include: the Chester Beatty Papyri I and II (late second-century ad; contains major portions of all four Gospels, Acts, and Paul's writings), the John Bodmer Papyri (175 ad, contains portions of Luke and John), p67 and p64 (125 to 150 ad; portions of Matthew's Gospel), and p4 (125 to 150 ad; a portion of Luke's Gospel). Possibly the oldest existing fragment of the New Testament is the John Rylands fragment of John chapter 18. It dates back to between 100 and 125 ad.[2] This is significant, since the earliest existing copies of Plato's writings date to about 1,200 years after Plato supposedly wrote.[3] With the New Testament, the earliest fragments we have date to within thirty years from when the originals were written. If we accept Plato's writings as authentic, then we are not justified in rejecting the New Testament documents.

Some scholars argue that there are about 200,000 errors in the thousands of manuscript copies we have today. However, these so called errors are merely "variants." Most are strictly grammatical (a difference in punctuation or spelling). Very few of the variants are considered significant. With so many copies of the New Testament in existence, we can compare the copies and figure out which variant reading is correct.

The great New Testament scholars of the nineteenth century, Westcott and Hort, argued that only one in sixty of these variants have any significance to the New Testament text. Hence, Westcott and Hort believed the New Testament text to be 98.33% pure. The great church historian Philip Schaff believed that only fifty variants had any real significance, and that not even one article of faith or moral command was called into question. The late Princeton scholar Bruce Metzger, due to his detailed studies of the manuscripts, argued that the New Testament text was 99.5% pure. With a text that pure, we have no question about what the original New Testament writings actually said about Jesus. Jesus' deity, His sacrificial death and bodily resurrection are never called into question by any of the ancient New Testament copies. His claims to be Savior and Messiah are also not in doubt.[4]

The evidence for the New Testament is so strong that just three of the Apostolic Fathers (i.e., pupils of the Apostles appointed by the Apostles to lead the early church) quote from or allude to twenty-five out of the twenty-seven books by 110 ad. These Apostolic Fathers were Clement of Rome, Polycarp, and Ignatius. Clearly, by 110 ad the leaders of the early church had no question as to which books belonged in the New Testament.[5] This is very important since the entire New Testament was written between the 30's ad and 100 ad. Most scholars would date the writings of the New Testament to between 50 ad and 100 ad.

Another Apostolic Father, named Papias, wrote that the Apostle Matthew originally wrote his Gospel in Hebrew, but that it was later translated into Greek. The early church fathers universally agreed that Matthew was the author of the first Gospel. Since Matthew had been a despised tax-collector, this is not something the early church would have fabricated. Matthew is frequently quoted by the Apostolic Fathers and the early church fathers. Hence, there is good evidence that Matthew the Apostle wrote the Gospel bearing his name.[6]

Papias also wrote that Mark was the Apostle Peter's scribe and that he wrote his Gospel based on Peter's preaching about the life and ministry of Jesus. The early church fathers are unanimous is ascribing the authorship of Mark's Gospel to Mark. Again, the early church had no incentive to lie about this. Mark was not one of the original apostles-why pretend he wrote a Gospel?[7]

The early church fathers agree that Luke, a companion of Paul, wrote both the Gospel of Luke and the Book of Acts.[8] Both writings are addressed to a man named Theophilus, with Acts being the sequel to Luke. Acts, which was written after Luke, speaks much about Peter, Paul, and James; yet, it inexplicitly does not record their deaths by martyrdom. Peter and Paul were executed in 64 to 67 ad, while James was stoned to death in Jerusalem in 62 ad. Also, it is strange that Acts does not record the Jewish War with the Romans (which began in 66 ad) or the destruction of the Jewish Temple (which occurred in 70 ad).

The only adequate explanation for leaving out these important details of the early church is that Luke wrote his Book of Acts before these events occurred. Hence, Luke wrote Acts before 62 ad (the death of James). This explains why Acts, a book which records many exciting events, ends anti-climatically with Paul in Rome, under house arrest, for two years. In fact, Acts closes at 61 ad. Therefore, Luke probably wrote about events right up to the present day (i.e., 61 ad) and then sent the Book of Acts to Theophilus.[9] The burden of proof is on anyone who wishes to argue for a later date for Acts. Since Luke was written before Acts, and Acts was written in 61 ad, Luke had to be written earlier-possibly in the 50's ad.

The early church fathers unanimously agreed that the Apostle John wrote the Gospel of John.[10] The oldest fragment of the New Testament comes form the eighteenth chapter of John (i.e., the John Rylands Papyri). Internal evidence from the Gospel shows details that only an eyewitness would know. This is why New Testament scholars like Richard Bauckham, even though he rejects that John the Apostle wrote this Gospel, admits it was written by an eyewitness who was a very close follower of Jesus.[11]

Seven of Paul's letters (Romans, 1 and 2 Corinthians, Gala-tians, Philippians, 1 Thessalonians, and Philemon) are excepted by nearly all New Testament scholars today.[12] If we appeal only to these undisputed writings of Paul, we see that Paul preached a Jesus who was crucified and rose from the dead. He proclaimed a Jesus who was fully God and fully man, a Jesus who is both Savior and Jewish Messiah. New Testament scholars agree that Paul wrote these letters between 49 and 64 ad. This means that they acknowledge that he began to write about Jesus less than twenty years after Jesus' death by crucifixion.

The Book of Hebrews was also written before 70 ad, the year the temple was destroyed. The unknown author was trying to convince his readers, who were Jews who accepted Jesus as Savior and Messiah, to persevere in the Christian faith. His readers were beginning to experience persecution and were thinking about leaving the Christian faith and returning to Judaism. The author of Hebrews argues that his readers should remain in the Christian fold and not return to Judaism. His argument is as follows: you should not return to the temple sacrifices since the temple priests are still "standing" and still "offering" animal sacrifices. If the bloodshed of animals took away sins, reasoned the author of Hebrews, the priests would be seated, their work would be done, and there would no longer be any need to offer more sacrifices. Jesus, on the other hand, is "seated" at the Father's right hand-His work is done. He offered Himself as the one sacrifice for the sins of all time-no further sacrifices are needed. Hence, argued the author of the Book of Hebrews, his readers should not return to Judaism since the priests are *still* offering sacrifices in the temple. Therefore, the temple was still standing; thus, the author wrote before 70 ad, the year the Romans destroyed the Jewish temple.[13]

If the author of Hebrews wrote after 70 ad, his argument would have been significantly different. He would have argued that his readers had nothing to return to—the temple had been destroyed! If God intended them to continue offering animal sacrifices for their sins, then why did God allow the pagans to destroy the temple? It is clear, based on the argument he used, that the author of Hebrews wrote before 70 ad, while the temple was still standing.

Based on the reliability of the books we have argued for (the four Gospels, Acts, seven of Paul's letters, and Hebrews), we have a strong base upon which to build a historical case for the Jesus of the Bible. All these books present Jesus as the crucified, risen Savior, the incarnate God and the Jewish Messiah. In the following two chapters, we will argue that the Jesus presented by these books is the true Jesus of history. But, we must first deal with the charge of the new atheists that the Bible contains contradicttions.

Several points should be noted when dealing with the accusation of contradictions in the Bible. First, as with all literature, the documents should be given the benefit of the doubt. The New Testament manuscripts should be considered true until proven false, not false until proven true. The new atheists assume contradictions and reject any possible reconciling of the passages.

Second, even if the New Testament contains contradictions (something I do not believe), that does not mean it cannot still be historically reliable. For instance, if the four Gospels contradicted each other concerning their accounts of the resurrection, these contradictions would not take from the fact that they agree on the empty tomb and the post-resurrection appearances of Jesus. The entire testimony of witnesses will not be thrown out in a court of law merely because of some discrepancies in the details.

Third, the supposed contradictions in the four Gospels actually point to their reliability rather than calling their reliability into question. Police officers and investigators become suspicious of witnesses that agree on every point-this usually points to collusion by the witnesses. The reliability of the testimonies is strengthened when at first glance there appears to be contradictions that are later reconciled.

Fourth, what first appear to be contradictions could be merely different perspectives or different emphases. There could be a rounding off of numbers, or a paraphrasing or summarizing of spoken words.

Fifth, the new atheists might err in their interpretation of the passages in question. They might simply misunderstand the passage or mistake figurative language for literal language (or vice versa).

Sixth, it is possible that the apparent contradiction might be due to errors in translation. The original Greek of the New Testament or the Hebrew of the Old Testament might reconcile the problem passages.

Finally, the doctrine of inerrancy only applies only to the original manuscripts which we no longer have. Hence, copyist errors might explain contradictory passages. As a conservative evangelical, I believe that every apparent contradiction found in the Bible can be explained through one of the seven points listed above. Anyone looking for possible, if not probable, resolutions to the Bible's apparent contradictions should refer to Geisler and Howe's *When Critics Ask* or Gleason Archer's *Encyclopedia of Bible Difficulties*.[14] The new atheists cannot find solutions to the apparent contradictions of the Bible because they do not want to find solutions.

ENDNOTES

1. Norman Geisler and Frank Turek, *I Don't Have Enough Faith to Be an Atheist* (Wheaton, Crossway Books, 2004), 225-228.
2. Craig A. Evans, *Fabricating Jesus* (Downers Grove: Inter Varsity press, 2006), 26, 28, 32-33.
3. Josh McDowell, *Evidence that Demands a Verdict* (San Bernardino: Here's Life Publishers, 1979), 42.
4. Geisler and Turek, 229.
5. Paul Barnett, *Is the New Testament Reliable?* (Downers Grove: Inter Varsity Press, 2003), 39-40.
6. John Wenham, *Redating Matthew, Mark, and Luke* (Downers Grove: Inter Varsity Press, 1992), 116-135.
7. Eusebius, *The Church History*. Translated with commentary by Paul L. Maier. (Grand Rapids: Kregel Publications, 1999), 129-130.
8. Wenham, 183-187.
9. Gregory Boyd, *Cynic Sage or Son of God?* (Wheaton: Bridgepoint Books, 1995), 253-256.
10. Henry Thiessen, *Introduction to the New Testament* (Grand Rapids: William B. Eerdmans Publishing Company, 1943), 162-173.
11. Richard Bauckham, *The Testimony of the Beloved Disciple* (Grand Rapids: Baker Book House, 2007).
12. Marcus Borg, *Jesus* (San Francisco: Harper Collins, 2006), 333.
13. Thiessen, 304.
14. Norman Geisler and Thomas Howe, *When Critics Ask* (Wheaton: Victor Books, 1992). Gleason L. Archer, *Encyclopedia of Bible Difficulties* (Grand Rapids: Zondervan Publishing House, 1982).

Chapter Eleven

Did Jesus Really Claim to be God?

Jesus claimed to be God incarnate, the Savior of mankind, and the Jewish Messiah. If Jesus bodily rose from the dead, then His resurrection confirms these claims about Himself to be true. He is indeed God the Son, the Savior, and the Jewish Messiah. We must now look at how we know He made these claims about Himself.

Jesus Claimed to be God

Numerous times in the New Testament, Jesus clearly claimed to be God. This is called explicit Christology. Many New Testament scholars reject Jesus' explicit claims to be God. These scholars believe that these New Testament passages were later placed on the lips of Jesus by the early church. In actuality, the only reason to reject these sayings of Jesus as authentic sayings of Christ is an a priori bias against miracles. (We have already shown this bias against the possibility of miracles to be misguided.) The manuscript evidence for the New Testament provides evidence that Jesus did make these claims. This is no early evidence for a non-supernatural Jesus-all the early evidence (i.e., between 30 ad and 100 ad) portrays Jesus as someone who thought of Himself as God incarnate.

The ancient creeds found in the New Testament predate the New Testament, some going back to the early 30's ad, and represent the teachings of the apostles themselves.[1] Several of these ancient creeds teach the deity of Christ (Philippians 2:5-11; Romans 10:9-10; 1 Timothy 3:16). Therefore, there is no reason to doubt that Jesus claimed to be God. The leaders of the first generation church taught that Jesus is God, and they were willing to die for their testimony. Hence, there is no reason (apart from an a priori bias against the supernatural) to reject the claims of deity made by Christ in the New Testament. The Jews understood that Jesus was claiming to be God:

> But He answered them, "My Father is working until now, and I myself am working." For this cause therefore the Jews were seeking all the more to kill Him, because He not only was breaking the Sabbath, but also was calling God His own Father, making Himself equal with God (John 5:17-18).

Whenever Jesus spoke of a unique Father-Son relationship between God the Father and Himself, the Jews understood Him to be claiming equality with God the Father. Jesus spoke to the Jews in their language. He communicated to them on their terms. They understood Jesus to be claiming to be deity. If Jesus never meant to claim to be God, then He was one of the poorest communicators who ever lived. If Jesus was misunderstood by His listeners, He should have clarified His words. A clear and articulate representtation of His words would have been in His best interest; He was executed for blasphemy (Mark 14:60-64). Jesus taught that He deserved the same honor that the Father deserved:

> For not even the Father judges anyone, But He has given all judgment to the Son, in order that all may honor the Son, even as they honor the Father. He who does not

honor the Son does not honor the Father who sent Him (John 5:22-23).

Since the Father is God, the honor due Him is worship. Therefore, Jesus taught that He also deserved to be worshiped. Despite the fact that the Old Testament Law forbid the worship of any being other than God (Exodus 20:1-6), Jesus accepted worship on numerous occasions (Matthew 2:11; 14:33; 28:9; John 9:38; 20:28-29). Jesus also stated:

> You are from below, I am from above; you are of this world, I am not of this world. I said therefore to you, that you shall die in your sins; for unless you believe that I am He, you shall die in your sins. . . . Truly, truly, I say to you, before Abraham was born, I am (John 8:23-24; 58).

The Jewish religious leaders understood Jesus' claim to deity in this passage: "they picked up stones to throw at Him" (John 8:59). The comments of J. Dwight Pentecost are helpful:

> Christ affirmed, "Before Abraham was born, I am!" (v. 58). "I AM" was the name of the Self-existing God who had revealed Himself to Moses at the burning bush (Exod. 3:14). Jesus Christ was claiming to be "I AM", the Self-existent God. He was claiming eternity. To the Jews this was blasphemy.[2]

Merrill C. Tenney also elaborates on this specific claim of Christ:

> In actuality the phrase "I am" is an assertion of absolute, timeless existence, not merely of a personal

identity as the English equivalent would suggest. A comparison of the use of the phrase, "I am" with self-revelation of Jehovah in the Old Testament shows that much the same terminology was employed. God, in commissioning Moses (Ex. 3:14), said: "Thus shalt thou say to unto the children of Israel, I AM hath sent me unto you." When the Jews heard Jesus say, "Before Abraham was born, I am," they took the statement to mean not priority to Abraham, but an assertion of deity. To them it was blasphemy, and they picked up stones to cast at Him.[3]

It is important to note two things about this passage. First, Jesus did not say, "Before Abraham was, I was." This would have been merely a claim to have preexisted Abraham. Though this would be a bold claim in itself, Christ actually said far more than that. Jesus was claiming that His existence is always in the present tense. In other words, He was claiming eternal existence for Himself. He was declaring himself to have absolutely no beginning. He was claiming that He was not bound by time. He was declaring Himself to be the eternal God. Second, Christ probably spoke these words in Aramaic (the common language of the Hebrews of his day) or Hebrew. Therefore, He probably did not use the Greek words "ego eimi" for "I AM." Rather, He would have used the Hebrew "YHWH." This was the title for the eternal God. Out of reverence for God, the Jews never spoke this word. So here, Christ was not only be speaking the unspeakable title of God (YHWH), but He was using it to refer to Himself. Properly understood, this was probably Christ's most unambiguous claim to deity. The Jews clearly understood this, and for this reason they attempted to stone him.

Another clear claim to deity made by Christ is the following passage:

"I and the Father are one." The Jews took up stones again to stone Him. Jesus answered them, "I showed you many good works from the Father; for which of them are you stoning Me?" The Jews answered Him, "For a good work we do not stone You, but for blasphemy; and because You, being a man, make yourself out to be God" (John 10:30-33).

Concerning this passage, Merrill F. Unger wrote, "Jesus asserted His unity of essence with the Father, hence His unequivocal deity. . . and the Jews understood Him."[4] In this passage, Jesus clearly claimed to be equal with God the Father. Christ said that His nature is identical to that of the Father. The Jews understood Him to be calling Himself God. They later sentenced Him to death for these claims to deity.

Jesus also made other claims to deity. He said that, "He who has seen Me has seen the Father" (John 14:9). When He prayed to the Father, He asked the Father to return to Him the glory which He and the Father shared before the universe was created (John 17:5). Yet, only God existed before creation, and God does not share His glory with another (Isaiah 42:8). Clearly, Jesus was claiming to be God.

The Apostles were Jesus' closest associates. They were more familiar with the teachings of Christ than anyone else and they called Jesus God (Matthew 1:23; John 1:1; John 20:28; Philippians 2:6; Colossians 2:9; Titus 2:13; 2 Peter 1:1). This is further confirmation that Jesus did in fact claim to be God.

Considering the strong evidence for the reliability of the New Testament, Christ's claims to deity cannot be considered as legends. The teaching that Jesus is God predates the New Testament (as shown in the ancient creeds), and is best explained by attributing the source of this doctrine to Jesus Himself. It must be remembered that the Apostles were not liars. They were sincere enough about their beliefs to die for them, and they recorded unambiguous statements made by Christ attributing deity to Himself.

The case for Jesus' deity based on His explicit claims is strong. Still, since many New Testament scholars throw out these explicit claims (for less than good reasons), we will now build a case for Jesus' deity on Jesus' implicit claims. Most New Testament scholars accept the statements below as authentic sayings of Jesus. However, these implicit claims of Jesus confirm His explicit claims; for, His implicit claims also show that Jesus considered Himself to be equal with God.

Larry Hurtado, a New Testament scholar who teaches at the University of Edinburgh, showed in his work *The Lord Jesus Christ* that when Paul began writing his letters in 49 or 50 ad, he already had a "high Christology." He already referred to Jesus as "the Lord Jesus Christ." He already equated Jesus with Yahweh-the God of the Old Testament. Yet, Paul mentioned Jesus' deity in passing-he did not argue for it. Hurtado observes that Paul like to debate. If there was any debate in the early church concerning the deity of Christ, Paul would have made the case for Jesus' deity. But, he does not. Instead, Paul assumes his readers (or any Christians in the 50's ad) accepted Christ's deity. Hurtado then notes that Paul claimed he taught the same gospel message that Peter, James, and John taught (Galatians 1 and 2). Hurtado then refers to ancient creeds and ancient sermons to solidify his case. He concludes that the early church, from its inception in the early 30's ad, engaged in "binitarian worship." In other words, before the early church figured out the role of the Holy Spirit and the doctrine of the Trinity, they came to realize Jesus' deity and began to worship Him as deity along side the Father. The early church was monotheistic-they believed in only one God. But, they acknowledged that, though Jesus was a distinct Person from the Father, He was also equally God-He shared the divine nature with the Father. Hence, Hurtado makes a strong case that the worship of Jesus as deity goes back to the early 30's ad-the start of the church.[5]

Many New Testament scholars acknowledge the "Son of Man" sayings as authentic sayings of Jesus. This is because of the critical principle called "discontinuity." This principle says that a saying attributed to Jesus in the Gospels was probably actually uttered by Jesus if it was dissimilar to what first-century ad Jews taught, and dissimilar to what the early church taught. The reasoning of critical scholars is that if the early church taught something, then they would place those words on Jesus' lips to give authority to their beliefs. But, this cannot apply to the "Son of Man" sayings. For, though the phrase comes from Daniel chapter seven, it was not in common use by the Jews of the first century ad. Also, the church almost never used the title of Jesus, not even in New Testament times. Yet, it was the most common title Jesus used of Himself. Hence, the principle of discontinuity shows that the "Son of Man" sayings were probably uttered by Jesus Himself.[6] But, when we look at the Son of Man sayings, we see several things that Jesus taught about Himself. Jesus predicted His death and resurrection numerous times (Mark 8:31; 9:31; 10:32-34). He claimed to be equal to God and have the power to forgive sins (Mark 2:5-12). Also, He claimed to be the Son of God and the Jewish Messiah, and He said that He would return to judge the world (Mark 14:61-64). He also claimed He came to earth to die "to give His life a ransom for many" (Mark 10:45). When Jesus called God "Abba," He claimed to have a closeness or intimacy with the Father that no one else had.[7] When He claimed that God was His "Abba" (something as intimate as "daddy," yet more respectful), the Jews understood Jesus to be claiming to be "the Son of God" and equal to God (John 5:17-18). Some modern critics reject the passages where Jesus called Himself the Son of God. But, it is hard for New Testament critics to deny the authenticity of Mark 13:32. For, in this passage, Jesus, while calling Himself "the Son," admits that, in His human nature, He did not know the day or the hour of His return. This is an excellent example of the principle of embarrassment. The Apostles would never place these words on the lips of Jesus if He did not actually say them, for they imply a limitation of Jesus' knowledge. Hence, Jesus did make this statement, and He did think of Himself as the Son of God.

Jesus viewed His interpretation of the Mosaic Law as holding as much authority as the Mosaic Law itself. He refused to quote from other rabbis for His authority, but instead (contrary to

137

the common practice of His day) He went right to the Old Testament and interpreted it Himself. His prefacing His interpretations with "truly, truly, I say to you" shows that He considered His interpretation of God's Law as authoritative as God's Law itself. Jesus implied that His interpretation of God's Law was as much God's Word as the Old Testament was.

Paul's accepted writings, the Gospel of Mark, the "Q" material (passages found in both Matthew and Luke, but not in Mark), the ancient sermons of Acts chapters one through twelve, and the ancient creeds all paint a portrait of Christ as God incarnate. Yet, even liberal New Testament critics agree that these sources all predate 70 ad. Hence, all the ancient evidence from the first generation ad points to a fully divine Jesus, without denying His true humanity.

Jesus Considered Himself the Savior of Mankind

Not only does the early evidence portray Jesus as God, but it also declares Him to be Savior and Messiah. Jesus taught that He was the Son of Man who would "give His life a ransom for many" (Mark 10:45). He taught that accepting or rejecting His teachings would determine a person's destiny (Matthew 7:24-27; Luke:6:47-49). Jesus said that those who acknowledged Him would be accepted in heaven; those who rejected Him would be rejected in heaven (Matthew 10:32-33; Luke 12:8-9). He said we could only know the Father if Jesus revealed Him to us (Matthew 10:27), that rest can only be found in Jesus (Matthew 11:28-29).

In the Gospel of John, Jesus explicitly taught that salvation comes only through faith in Him (John 3:16-18; 6:35, 47; 11:25-26; 14:6). At the Last Supper, Jesus claimed His body would be broken and His blood would be shed for the sins of mankind so that we could be forgiven (Matthew 26:26-28). Clearly, Jesus claimed to be the Savior of mankind.

The Apostles, Jesus closest followers, also taught that salvation comes only through faith in Jesus. Paul proclaimed salvation to be by God's grace alone through faith alone in Jesus alone (Ephesians 1:7; 2:8-9; Romans 3:10, 20-28; 5:8-10; 6:23; 10:4, 9, 13; Galatians 1:3-4; 3:24-26). The author of Hebrews also teaches salvation through Jesus' death on the cross (Hebrews 10:10-14), as does the Apostle Peter (1 Peter 2:24; 3:18). Surely, the earliest evidence indicates that Jesus and His Apostle taught that Jesus is the Savior of the world.

Jesus Considered Himself the Jewish Messiah

Not only does all the pre-70 ad evidence and the first century evidence portray Jesus as God and Savior, but it also declares Him to be the Jewish Messiah. If, as liberal scholars contend, the early church was willing to put their teachings on the lips of Jesus then, since the early church proclaimed Jesus to be the Jewish Messiah, they would have had Jesus call Himself the Messiah on many occasions. But, this is not the case. Jesus' favorite title for Himself was "the Son of Man," not the Messiah. This is because the first century Jews were expecting a military, conquering Messiah. Jesus wanted to take the focus off of military conquest and place it on spiritual redemption. Hence, He called Himself the Son of Man so that He could define His ministry in His own terms. Still, He admitted to Peter, the Samaritan woman, and the Jewish High Priest that He is the Jewish Messiah (Matthew 16:13-17; John 4:25-26; Mark 14:61-64). Had the early church fabricated Jesus' claim to be Messiah, the Gospels would record Jesus claiming to be Messiah in public on numerous occasions.

Why the Gnostic Texts were Rejected

Many contemporary popular writers reject this first century ad portrait of Jesus as God, Savior, and Messiah. Instead, they proclaim Jesus as somewhat of a guru who imparted secret knowledge to His followers. This was the false Jesus of the Gnostic writings.

The Gnostic writings were rejected by the early church for numerous reasons. First, the Gnostic writings (i.e., the Gospel of Judas, the Gospel of Thomas, the Gospel of Philip, the Gospel of Mary, etc.) were written much too late. The earliest possible date given to some of these books is about 140 ad, over one-hundred years after Jesus' death and resurrection. Hence, they lacked apostolic authority and did not come from eyewitnesses or anyone who personally knew the eyewitnesses. Hence, the information was written far too late to contain reliable information about Jesus and His teachings.

Second, these writings were deceptive. They are often classified as pseudepigrapha because they were forgeries. The unknown authors were not the persons they claimed to be. No New Testament critic, not even the liberal critics of the Jesus Seminar, believes that these books were actually written by Judas, Thomas, Philip, or Mary Magdalene. The authors were lying; they claimed to be someone they were not.

Third, the Gnostic writings were considered heretical by the early church, and therefore could not be added to the canon. The Gnostics rejected salvation through faith in Jesus and instead taught salvation through secret knowledge. (The word "Gnosticism" comes from the Greek word "gnosis" which means knowledge.) The ancient Gnostics rejected the Old Testament as an evil book written by an evil god. They taught that matter is totally evil and the spiritual realm is totally good. Since the Old Testament God created the material universe, the Gnostics deemed Him to be an evil god. Whereas biblical Christianity has always considered itself to be the completion or fulfillment of the Jewish

Faith (i.e., the Old Testament), the Gnostics were opposed to the teachings of the Old Testament and the God of the Jewish Faith. Hence, the early church rejected the Gnostic writings as being heretical; these writings were not in agreement with previous revelation. Hence, as heretical works, the early church believed the Gnostic texts were not edifying for true believers. Since God inspired or guided the early church to write His Word, He also guided the early church to recognize which books belonged in the canon (i.e., the list of books which belonged in the Bible). The Gnostic writings were written too late to be authoritative records of Jesus' ministry and life. They were heretical, and they were forgeries. There was and is no reason to include the Gnostic writings in the New Testament. The Jesus of the Gnostic writings is a false Jesus. The Gnostic Jesus is not the true Jesus of history.

Christianity did not Borrow from Ancient Myths

Many critics of Christianity claim that Jesus is just another ancient myth. These skeptics believe that the early church borrowed from ancient pagan myths-the early church was not really recording any reliable information about the true Jesus of history. Two Christian scholars who have effectively responded to this objection to Christianity are Ronald Nash (author of *The Gospel and the Greeks*)[8] and J. P. Moreland (author of *Scaling the Secular City*).[9] As we refute the myth hypothesis in this chapter, we will discuss the defense of the historicity of Jesus made by these two scholars.

Nash and Moreland point out that there are numerous differences between the New Testament information about Jesus and the ancient myths. First, there is a long gap in time between the first writing down of ancient myths and the time when that myth supposedly occurred. In fact, in most cases the subject of the myth is not even a historical person or event. In the case of the New Testament Jesus, the entire New Testament was written during a time when eyewitnesses who knew Jesus were still alive and leading the church. The entire New Testament should be dated to the first century ad. In fact, ancient creeds (Colossians 1:15-17; Philippians 2:5-11; Romans 10:9; 2 Corinthians 5:15; etc.) that speak of Jesus' deity, resurrection, and substitutionary death probably go back to the decade in which Jesus died-the 30's ad. As the historian and expert on ancient mythology, A. N. Sherwin-White has stated, legends or myths need at least two generations to get started and gain acceptance.[10] With the New Testament portrait of Jesus, there is simply not enough time for a myth to have developed—the Jesus of the Gospels is the true Jesus of history.

Second, usually myths that sound like forerunners of Christianity were actually written after the New Testament writings were complete. Hence, if borrowing occurred, it was probably mythology that borrowed from Christianity. It is difficult, if not impossible, to identify pre-Christian myths that depict a full-blown incarnation, death, and resurrection. When myths take on these ideas, it seems that they post-date Christianity.[11]

Third, the mystery religions were syncretistic—their adherents liked to blend beliefs from other religions with their own beliefs. Christianity, on the other hand, like the Judaism from which it came, was very exclusive. The early church, like first century Judaism, did not borrow from other religions. The early church believed that all non-Christian religions were false and that salvation comes only through Jesus. In short, the early church was not inclined to borrow from the pagan religions and their myths.

Fourth, J. P. Moreland points out that the similarities between the Gospels and the pagan myths are often exaggerated by skeptics.[12] In fact, often the myths only look similar to the Gospel if we use Christian terminology to describe them or read Christian themes into these myths.

Fifth, the ancient mystery religions had more concern about the religious experiences or emotional states of their followers than for correct doctrine. Early Christianity, conversely, had a large emphasis on history and correct doctrine—its focus was not primarily on the subjective state of its adherents.

Sixth, the writers of the ancient myths did not write as if they expected their readers to take them literally. Yet, the Gospel authors wrote as if they were recording real history. They informed their readers concerning the identity of current leaders, the time of the year, descriptions of the location, and other key factors which would enable the reader to place the events in their proper historical, chronological, and geographical setting. This is not the case with the ancient myths.[13]

Seventh, the vast majority of the world's leading New Testament scholars no longer try to trace the origin of Christianity to pagan myths. It is now widely accepted by New Testament scholarship that the ancient Jewish Faith is the root of New Testament Christianity, not Greek and Roman mythology.

Concerning myths, two important points made by C. S. Lewis should be mentioned. C. S. Lewis was open to the possibility that some of the ancient myths of a God-man Savior who dies and rises may predate biblical Christianity. But Lewis saw this, even if true, as no obstacle to Christian belief. Lewis believed the first preaching of the Gospel was found in the Garden of Eden just after Adam and Eve fell into sin. God promised that a man would be born of woman ("the seed of the woman") who would save mankind by defeating Satan (the one who spoke through the serpent), but would be bruised in the process (Genesis 3:15). Therefore, reasoned Lewis, all of ancient mankind had some remembrance of the promise of a coming, suffering Savior who would redeem mankind from the curse.

Also, Lewis appreciated God's revelation to mankind through nature. Hence, the four seasons may have been given to mankind as a hint of the coming redeemer. In the Winter, nature dies, but it is reborn or resurrected in the Spring. Many of the ancient myths had to do with the seasons and the production of crops. Yet, God may have given ancient pagans hints about the coming redeemer, so that when He came, died, and rose, He would fulfill the hope of many pagans who were living in the expectancy of a dying and rising God. Lewis viewed the ancient myths as

143

"signposts" pointing to the day when God would become a man, die for our sins, and rise from the dead.[14]

Although Lewis viewed the incarnation (God the Son becoming a man) as the myth that came true, he also noted that the Gospels were written as if the authors were recording straightforward history, not mythology. In other words, as an expert on ancient mythology, Lewis realized that the Gospels were not even written in the genre (or literary style) of mythology. They were written as if recording ancient history.[15]

The Jesus found on the pages of the New Testament is not a myth, nor was He borrowed from ancient myths. The New Testament was written by reliable eyewitnesses who were sincere enough about their beliefs that they were willing to suffer and die for their beliefs. They were not telling stories. The Gospel writers did not borrow from ancient myths. They reported accurately what they saw and heard concerning Jesus. Men do not die for legends or myths; the apostles were willing to suffer and die for Jesus because they witnessed His miracles and His post-resurrection appearances. They saw Him fulfill numerous Old Testament prophecies of the coming Messiah. They believed His claims to be God, Messiah, and Savior. Hence they were willing to die for Jesus-the true Jesus of history, not a mythological, fairy-tale Jesus. Hence, Paul could make a clear distinction between such things as "sound doctrine" and "truth," and the "myths" or fables of false teachers (2 Timothy 4:3-4). As the Apostle Peter wrote, "For we did not follow cleverly devised tales when we made known to you the power and coming of our Lord Jesus Christ, but we were eyewitnesses of His majesty" (2 Peter 1:16).

ENDNOTES

1. Gary Habermas, *The Historical Jesus* (Joplin, MD: College Press, 1996), 143-157.
2. J. Dwight Pentecost, *The Words and Works of Jesus Christ* (Grand Rapids: Academie Books, 1981), 288.
3. Merrill C. Tenney, *John, the Gospel of Belief* (Grand Rapids: William B. Eerdmans Publishing Company, 1948), 150.
4. Merrill F. Unger, *Unger's Bible Handbook* (Chicago: Moody Press, 1966), 555.
5. Larry Hurtado, *The Lord Jesus Christ* (Grand Rapids: William B. Eerdmans Publishing Company, 2003), 101, 128-129, 131-133, 174-176, 650.
6. Gary Habermas, *The Risen Jesus and Future Hope* (Lanham, MD: Rowman and Littlefield Publishers, 2003), 100-106.
7. Ibid., 107.
8. Ronald Nash, *The Gospel and the Greeks* (Phillipsburg, NJ: P & R Publishing, 2003).
9. J. P. Moreland, *Scaling the Secular City* (Grand Rapids: Baker Book House, 1987), 181-183.
10. A. N. Sherwin-White, *Roman Society and Roman Law in the New Testament* (Oxford: Clarendon, 1963), 188-191.
11. Moreland, 182.
12. Ibid.
13. Ibid.
14. Armand M. Nicholi, Jr. *The Question of God* (New York: The Free Press, 2002), 86-90, 232. C. S. Lewis, *Miracles* (New York: Collier Books, 1960), 133-134.
15. Nicholi, 86.

Chapter Twelve

Did Jesus Really Rise From the Dead?

There is strong evidence that Jesus of Nazareth bodily rose from the dead. If Jesus rose from the dead this would confirm His teachings to be true—He is God, Savior, and Messiah. We will now look at the historical evidence for Jesus' bodily resurrection from the dead. The new atheists, due to their bias against the possibility of miracles, have not looked into the historical evidence for Christ's resurrection. Dawkins and Hitchens are too closed-minded to look into the evidence-their minds are already made up. Rather than examine the evidence for Christ's resurrection, they instead ridicule those who believe Jesus rose. While claiming to be scientific, the new atheists name call and belittle, rather than dealing with the evidence.

Dr. Gary Habermas of Liberty University has researched the issue of Jesus' resurrection probably more than any other contemporary scholar. He has read everything in print, in English, German, and French, from the world's leading New Testament scholars, written from 1975 to the present day. Habermas was able to chart their views concerning the resurrection.[1]

His work shows that the vast majority of New Testament scholars (i.e., over 97%) acknowledge, based on the New Testament evidence, that 1) Jesus died by crucifixion, 2) his apostles' lives were transformed by what they believed were appearances to them of the resurrected Jesus, 3) Paul's life was transformed by what he believed was a post-resurrection appearance of Jesus, and 4) James' life was somehow transformed from being a mocker of His brother to being one of the key leaders in the early church. Habermas also shows that over 70% of the world's leading New Testament scholars acknowledge that the tomb was found empty early Sunday morning after Christ's crucifixion.[2] Habermas believes that the best explanation of the accepted data is that Jesus did in fact rise from the dead and appear to His disciples.

The strength of Habermas' argument for Jesus' resurrection is in the fact that he uses what the world's leading critical New Testament scholars accept to build his case for the historicity of Jesus' bodily resurrection. Most of these critics start their research with a strong bias against the resurrection. Using highly critical principles (i.e., multiple attestation, embarrassment, discontinuity, enemy attestation, etc.), these scholars have uncovered solid historical data that they feel compelled to accept. That is the data that Gary Habermas uses to prove Jesus' resurrection.

In the case of *the empty tomb*, further argumentation is needed. This is because only just over 70% of New Testament scholars accept the empty tomb, rather than the near universal support for the other four pieces of data. There are several reasons which show that the accounts of the empty tomb are probably historical. First, the first eyewitnesses of the empty tomb (and the resurrected Christ) were women. This is something the apostles would not have made up, for a woman's testimony was held highly suspect in the first-century ad. It offered practically no evidential value to fabricate a story of women being the first witnesses.[3] Plus, the principle of embarrassment applies here. For, it would have been very embarrassing for the two leading apostles, Peter and John, to have been proven wrong by ladies. This would be horrible public relations for the early church. The only reason for reporting that women were the first witnesses of the empty tomb would be if it was actually true.

Second, if Jesus did not rise from the dead, then the Jewish religious authorities would have produced the rotting corpse of Christ, thus refuting Christianity and stifling its growth at its earliest stage. But this did not happen—Christianity grew at a tremendous rate in the early 30's ad in the Jerusalem area. This would not be the case if Jesus' body was still in the tomb.

Third, New Testament scholars agree that the sermons of Acts chapter 1 through 12 are the earliest sermons of the church- they date back to the early 30's ad. Their antiquity is accepted by scholars because these sermons show no signs of theological development (this type of theological development is found in Paul's letters which were written twenty years later).[4] These sermons seem to report the events of the resurrection at the earliest stage of the church. One of the main themes of these early sermons was the resurrection of Jesus. Hence, the resurrection of Jesus was reported shortly after Christ's crucifixion by people who claimed to be eyewitnesses and who were willing to suffer and die for their proclamation. Men do not die for what they know to be a hoax- they sincerely believed they saw the risen Christ.

Fourth, Jesus was buried in the tomb of a well-known man- Joseph of Arimathea. It would have been easy to locate the tomb to ascertain if it was empty. Many critics acknowledge the reliability of the account of Jesus being buried in Joseph's tomb.[5] For, if there was no real Joseph of Arimathea on the Jewish Ruling Council, then this account would be easily refuted by the enemies of the early church. However, once we admit that there existed a man named Joseph of Arimathea on the Jewish Ruling Council, then it is highly unlikely the apostles fabricated this account. Joseph would have been easy to find-there were only 70 members on the Sanhedrin and they met regularly in Jerusalem. If the apostles lied about the burial, then one could interview Joseph of Arimathea to check the account to disprove it. But, once we admit Jesus was buried in the tomb of a famous man, then we must acknowledge how easy it would have been to prove the corpse was still in the tomb, had it actually been there. But, this did not happen. Hence, the tomb was empty.

The ancient creed found in 1 Corinthians 15:3-8 also provides strong evidence of the post-resurrection appearances of Jesus to His followers. In the Apostle Paul's First Letter to the Corinthians, we find excellent eyewitness testimony concerning the resurrection that nearly dates back to the event itself. The Apostle Paul wrote:

> For I delivered to you as of first importance what I also received, that Christ died for our sins according to the Scriptures, and that He was buried, and that He was raised on the third day according to the Scriptures, and that He appeared to Cephas, then to the twelve. After that He appeared to more than five hundred brethren at one time, most of whom remain until now, but some have fallen asleep; then He appeared to James, then to all the apostles; and last of all, as it were to one untimely born, He appeared to me also (1 Corinthians 15:3-8).

Most New Testament scholars, liberal and conservative alike, agree that this passage is an ancient creed or hymn formulated by the early church.[6] In our task of ascertaining when the creed of 1 Corinthians 15 was created, it is first necessary to determine when Paul wrote 1 Corinthians. In this way, we will establish the latest possible date for the creed. We can then work our way back in time from that date, following any clues based upon the internal evidence found in the creed itself.

Christian philosopher J. P. Moreland has correctly stated that for the past one hundred years almost all New Testament critics have accepted the Pauline authorship of 1 Corinthians.[7] A comparison of 1 Corinthians 16 with Acts 18, 19, and 20 provides strong evidence that 1 Corinthians was written by Paul in 55AD while in Ephesus.[8] Scholars such as John A. T. Robinson, Henry C. Thiessen, A. T. Robertson, Douglas Moo, Leon Morris, and D. A. Carson all concur that 1 Corinthians was written in the mid 50's AD.[9]

If 55AD is the approximate date for the composition of 1 Corinthians, then the ancient creed quoted by Paul in 1 Corinthians 15:3-8 had to originate before this date. However, there is strong evidence found in the creed itself that points to its development at a much earlier time.

Christian apologist Gary Habermas discusses at least eight pieces of evidence from within the creed that indicate a very early date.[10] First, the terms "delivered" and "received" have been shown to be technical rabbinic terms used for the passing on of sacred tradition. Second, Paul admitted that this statement was not his own creation and that he had received it from others. Third, scholars agree that some of the words in the creed are non-Pauline terms and are clearly Jewish. These phrases include "for our sins," "according to the Scriptures," "He has been raised," "the third day," "He was seen," and "the twelve." Fourth, the creed is organized into a stylized and parallel form; it appears to have been an oral creed or hymn in the early church. Fifth, the creed shows evidence of being of a Semitic origin and, thus, points to a source that predates Paul's translation of it into Greek. This can be seen in the use of "Cephas" for Peter, for "Cephas" is Aramaic for Peter (which is Petros in the Greek). Moreland notes additional evidence for the Semitic origin of this creed by relating that the poetic style of the creed is clearly Hebraic.[11] Sixth, Habermas reasons that Paul probably received this creed around 36-38AD, just three years after his conversion, when he met with Peter and James in Jerusalem (as recorded by Paul in Galatians 1:18-19). Jesus' death occurred around 30AD, and Paul was converted between 33 and 35AD. Seventh, Habermas states that, due to the above information, "numerous critical theologians" date the creed "from three to eight years after Jesus' crucifixion."[12] Eighth, since it would have taken a period of time for the beliefs to become formalized into a creed or hymn, the beliefs behind the creed must date back to the event itself.

As mentioned above, the antiquity of this creed is almost universally accepted across the theological spectrum of New Testament scholarship. A brief list of some of the world's leading New Testament scholars, past and present, who date the origin of this creed to the early 30's ad (just a few years after the crucifixion) will suffice: Gerd Luedemann, Marcus Borg, Reginald Fuller, Oscar Cullman, Wolfhart Panneberg, Martin Hengel, Hans

Conzelman, C. H. Dodd. A. M. Hunter, James Dunn, N. T. Wright, Richard Bauckham, Rudolph Bultmann, Raymond E. Brown, Larry Hurtado, Joachim Jeremias, Norman Perrin, George E. Ladd, and Willi Marxsen.[13] Again, this list of New Testament scholars covers the theological spectrum. Some are evangelical, or at least fairly conservative in their theology and view of the Bible, while others are rather liberal in their theological and biblical perspective. Virtually, all the world's leading New Testament scholars, despite their theological perspectives, date this creed to the early 30's ad.

We have provided strong evidence that the creed of 1 Corinthians 15:3-8 originated between three to eight years after Christ's crucifixion, and that the beliefs which underlie this creed must therefore go back to the event itself. Now we must briefly examine the content of this ancient creed.

First, the creed, as stated in this passage, mentions the death and burial of Christ. Second, it states that Christ was raised on the third day. Third, it lists several post-resurrection appearances of Christ. These include appearances to Peter, to the twelve apostles, to over 500 persons at one time, to James (the Lord's brother), to all the apostles, and, finally an appearance to Paul himself.

It should be noted that scholars differ as to the exact contents of this ancient creed in its most primitive form. I believe that Paul added verse eight (detailing his own eyewitness account) to the original creed, as well as a portion of verse six (a reminder that most of the 500 witnesses were still alive). This in no way lessons the force of this ancient creed. In fact, it strengthens it as evidence for the resurrection, for Paul adds his own testimony and encourages his readers to question the many eyewitnesses still living in his day. Even scholars who disagree with my view still accept a large enough portion of the creed for it to be considered a valuable piece of eyewitness evidence for the resurrection of Christ from the dead.

Having argued for a very early date for its origin, we must now ascertain the evidential value of this creed. Simply stated, the early date of the 1 Corinthians 15 creed proves that the resurrection accounts found in the New Testament are not legends. Christian philosopher William Lane Craig, while commenting on the work of the great Roman historian A. N. Sherwin-White, stated that "even two generations is too short a time span to allow legendary tendencies to wipe out the hard core of historical facts."[14] If two generations is not enough time for legends to develop, then there is no way that a resurrection legend could emerge in only three to eight years.

It should also be noted that, in this creed, Paul is placing his apostolic credentials on the line by encouraging his Corinthian critics to check out his account with the eyewitnesses who were still alive. These eyewitnesses not only included over 500 people, but also Peter, James, and the other apostles-the recognized leaders of the early church (Galatians 2:9). It is highly improbable that Paul would fabricate the creed and jeopardize his own position in the early church.

Finally, it should be obvious to any open-minded person who examines the evidence that Paul was a man of integrity. He was not lying. Not only did he put his reputation and position in the early church on the line, but he was also willing to suffer and die for Christ. Men do not die for what they know to be a hoax. Paul was a reliable and sincere witness to the resurrection of Christ.

Hence, the creed of 1 Corinthians 15:3-8 provides us with reliable eyewitness testimony for the bodily resurrection of Jesus Christ. Not only did Paul testify that he had seen the risen Christ, but he also identified many other witnesses to the resurrection that could have been interrogated. Contrary to the futile speculations of liberal scholars, Paul was not devising myths behind closed doors. No, from the beginning he was preaching a risen Savior who had conquered death and the grave, a risen Savior who had met him on the road to Damascus and changed his life forever.

The ancient creed of 1 Corinthians 15:3-8 is an example of the type of evidence that has convinced virtually all the world's leading New Testament scholars that the lives of the apostles, Paul, and James (the brother of Jesus) were radically transformed by what they believed were post-resurrection appearances of Jesus. Scholars agree that the apostles were transformed from cowardly men who fled and hid on the night Jesus was executed to courageous men willing to suffer and die for Christ. They proclaimed Jesus as the Jewish Messiah; yet, Jesus died before Israel was delivered from her pagan enemies-the Romans. When a self-proclaimed Messiah dies, his movement dies with him. When Jesus died, His Messiah movement died as well. Yet, fifty days later, at the Feast of Pentecost, it came back to life. Since a dead Messiah cannot rescue Israel from her enemies, the Messiah must have come back to life as well. The resurrection strengthened the faith of the apostles to the point that they were willing to suffer and die for Jesus.

New Testament scholars agree that Paul was a leading persecutor of the early church. However, within a few years of the crucifixion, he was radically changed. The persecutor of the church became its greatest missionary and theologian, and one of its greatest leaders. Only Jesus' post-resurrection appearance to Paul on the Road to Damascus (Acts 9) adequately explains this radical transformation, a transformation that led to much suffering and, eventually, martyrdom by beheading.

James was an orthodox Jew and one of Jesus' brothers. During Jesus' public ministry, James was not a believer. In fact, he mocked his brother and may have even questioned his brother's sanity (John 7:3-5; Mark 3:31-35; 6:3; Mt 13:55). This is embarrassing material-the Gospels would not report this rejection of Jesus by His brothers unless it was true. Yet, in less than fifty days after the crucifixion, James became one of the most respected leaders in Jesus' church (Acts 1:14; Galatians 1:18-19; 2:9). What brought about such a drastic and abrupt change? Only Jesus' resurrection and appearance to James adequately explains how the mocking brother became a bold and courageous follower of his brother. In 62 ad, James was stoned to death for preaching his brother Jesus was the Jewish Messiah.

We must also remember that when we speak of Jesus' resurrection, we are talking about a *bodily resurrection*. Many people misunderstand Paul's phrase "spiritual body" in 1 Corinthians 15. They mistake this phrase for signifying some type of immaterial spirit. However, this is not the case. In the Greek, the phrase is "soma pneumatikon." The word soma almost always refers to a physical body. Still, in this passage this physical body is somehow described as being "spiritual" (pneumatikon). But, the spiritual body is contrasted with the natural body. The natural body refers to the physical body before physical death. The Greek words for natural body are "soma psuchikon." Literally, this phrase means a "soulish body." The word soul usually carries with it the idea of immateriality, but, in this passage, it cannot. It is referring to the human body before death, and, the human body is of course physical, despite the adjective "soulish." Therefore, if the "soulish body" is physical, then there should be no difficulty viewing the "spiritual body" as also being physical. The soulish body is sown (buried) at death, but, this same body is raised as a spiritual body; it receives new powers. It is no longer a natural body; it is a supernatural body. The body is changed, but it is still the same body. For, the body that was sown (buried) is the same body that will be raised. Gary Habermas discussed Christ's spiritual body in the following words: the Gospels and Paul agree on an important fact: the resurrected Jesus had a new spiritual body. The Gospels never present Jesus walking out of the tomb. . . when the stone is rolled away, Jesus does not walk out the way He does in apocryphal literature. He's already gone, so He presumably exited through the rock. Later He appears in buildings and then disappears at will. The Gospels clearly say that Jesus was raised in a spiritual body. It was His real body, but it was changed, including new, spiritual qualities.[15]

Paul is using the term spiritual body to contrast it with the natural body. He is making the point that Christ's body after the resurrection (and ours too) has different characteristics to it than it did before. . . But the point is made very clearly that what is being talked about is the

155

same body, the contrast here is not between physical body and spiritual body, but rather between the same body in different states or with different characteristics.[16]

Walter Martin, the foremost authority on non-Christian cults during his lifetime, also discussed Christ's spiritual body in his greatest work, *Kingdom of the Cults*:

> However, Christ had a "spiritual body" (1 Corinthians 15:50, 53) in His glorified state, identical in form to His earthly body, but immortal, and thus capable of entering the dimension of earth or heaven with no violation to the laws of either one.[17]

Therefore, Christ rose in the same body in which He lived and died. However, His body had been changed in the "twinkling of an eye" (1 Corinthians 15:50-53) so that His mortal body (a body capable of death) was glorified and became immortal (incapable of death). In His spiritual body, He can apparently travel at the speed of thought, unhindered by distance. The Bible teaches that in the first resurrection all believers will receive glorified bodies. Believers' bodies will be changed into glorified and immortal bodies. The presence of sin will be totally removed from them (1 Corinthians 15:50-53).

There are several good arguments that Jesus' resurrection was bodily-it was not merely a spiritual resurrection. First, as the British New Testament scholar N. T, Wright points out, the Greek words for resurrection (anistemi, anastasis, eigero, etc.), in the first century ad, always meant a reanimation of a corpse, the raising back to life of a dead body. Even those who denied the reality of resurrection always used these words to refer to bodily resurrection when denying the reality of resurrection.[18]

Second, Paul was a Pharisee (Philippians 3:5). The Pharisees believed in the concept of physical resurrection—they believed that the children of God would be bodily raised from the dead on the last day. A non-bodily resurrection is an oxymoron.

Third, Paul believed in life after death, and that life after death started immediately following death for the believer (2 Corinthians 5:8; Philippians 1:23). But, resurrection is something that occurred *after* life after death. For instance, the creed of 1 Corinthians 15:3-8 states that Jesus died, was buried, and then was raised "on the third day" (vs. 4). So, as N. T. Wright says, resurrection is "life after life-after-death." The difference between life after death and life after life-after-death is that the former is non-bodily existence, while the latter is bodily existence. Hence, the first-century ad concept of resurrection was bodily.[19]

Fourth, the Old Testament concept of resurrection (Daniel 12; Ezekiel 37; Isaiah 26:19), which was inherited by the early church, was clearly that of bodily resurrection. Fifth, Paul's writings reveal that when he spoke of resurrection he meant bodily resurrection (1 Thessalonians 4:13-18; Philippians 3:21). Sixth, 1 Corinthians 15:42-44, speaking about the resurrection body, says that that which is sown or buried is that which is raised-the same thing that is buried (i.e., the body) is the same thing that is raised (i.e., the body). Seventh, if Paul denied the bodily resurrection and was trying to proclaim a spiritual resurrection, why not say "it is sown a soma (body), but it is raised a pneuma (spirit)?"

And, finally, the Gospel accounts of Jesus post-resurrection appearances, according to N. T. Wright, are not very theologically developed. These accounts are certainly much less theologically developed than Paul's discussions of Jesus' resurrection in his letters. Paul draws a lot of theological data from Jesus' resurrection-this implies he thought deeply about the theological implications of Jesus' resurrection. This is not the case in the Gospels—the resurrection and appearances are merely reported as historical incidents. Wright argues that this shows that the resurrection accounts in the Gospels predate Paul's writings. Since Paul began to write around 50 ad, the Gospel accounts of Jesus' resurrection and appearances must predate 50 ad.[20] Yet, in these early accounts, Jesus is reported to have bodily appeared to His disciples. He still had the scars in His hands, feet, and side. He encouraged the apostles to touch Him; He even ate food with them (John 20:26-29; Luke 24: 36-43). Together, these eight points make it clear that the early church proclaimed and believed that Jesus bodily rose from the dead.

One final issue needs to be mentioned to seal the case for Christ's bodily resurrection: the failure of naturalistic theories. All alternative, non-supernatural explanations of the resurrection data fail to explain the almost universally accepted data we have mentioned. This is why the naturalistic theories of Jesus' resurrection are not popular today-they fail to explain the agreed-upon data.

The stolen body theory fails because the disciples were sincere enough in their belief that Jesus rose from the dead that they were willing to die for that belief. Men do not die for what they know to be a hoax; hence, the disciples did not steal the body and fabricate the resurrection accounts.

But what if others stole the body without the disciples' knowledge? This would explain the empty tomb, but not the experiences the apostles had in which they believe they saw the risen Christ numerous times. The stolen body theory simply does not adequately explain the historical data accepted by the vast majority of New Testament scholars.

The wrong tomb theory fails. This alternative "explanation" speculates that maybe the women went to the wrong tomb and found it empty. They then told the disciples, who visited the same wrong tomb, also finding it empty. As a result, the disciples mistakenly proclaimed Jesus as risen from the dead. This alternative explanation fails due to the fact that the empty tomb alone did not convince the disciples that Jesus rose. They were persuaded that Jesus rose from the dead when they had experiences in which they believed He appeared to them alive from the dead. The wrong tomb theory does not explain the apostles' experiences of the post-resurrection Christ.

The swoon theory is the idea that maybe Jesus merely passed out on the cross; He did not actually die. Maybe, He was revived in the tomb and was some how able to remove the large stone covering the mouth of the tomb. He then somehow traveled on scarred feet on rocky ground and appeared to His disciples. They mistook Him for risen and proclaimed Him as the Lord. This explanation fails for several reasons. First, the Roman soldier confirmed Jesus was dead with his spear thrust to Jesus' side. The Romans would confirm death before removing bodies from crosses. Second, due to the rigors of the Roman scourging and crucifixion, assuming Jesus was alive in the tomb, He would have almost certainly died due to His wounds while staying in a cold, damp tomb. Third, John records that when Jesus' side was pierced, blood and water flowed from His side. Modern medical science has proven that this only happens when the side of a corpse has been punctured-Jesus was already dead when His side was pierced. Fourth, even if we ignore all the above evidence against the swoon theory, it is hard to believe that the apostles would have seen Jesus in His dire, unhealthy state, and then proclaim Him as the risen Savior who has conquered death! No, they would have sought medical attention for a severely beaten, dying friend. For these reasons and others, virtually no scholars promote the swoon theory today.

Finally, the hallucination theory also fails to adequately explain the resurrection data. This view supposes that the apostles never saw the risen Christ; they merely hallucinated on numerous occasions, thinking they had seen Jesus alive from the dead. There are many problems with this theory. First, hallucinations occur inside a person's mind. Hence, no two people (let alone the apostles or over 500 people at one time) can share the same hallucination. Yet, Jesus appeared to groups of people on numerous occasions. Second, people who have hallucinations are easily convinced by others that they are mistaken. They are certainly not willing to suffer and die for their hallucinations. Third, the hallucination theory does not explain the empty tomb. Since there is good evidence for the empty tomb, this also counts against the hallucination theory. Once again, few scholars today entertain the hallucination theory. Therefore, the most historically plausible explanation for the data in question is that Jesus of Nazareth did in fact bodily rise from the dead.

Jesus Taught the Old Testament is God's Inerrant Word

Jesus' resurrection from the dead proves His claims to be God, Savior, and Jewish Messiah are true. Therefore, whatever Jesus taught should be accepted as true and authoritative. John W. Wenham discussed Christ's view of the Old Testament:

Our Lord not only believed the truth of the Old Testament history and used the Scriptures as final authority in matters of faith and conduct, he also regarded the writings themselves as inspired. To Him, Moses, the prophets, David, and the other Scripture writers were given their messages by the Spirit of God.[21]

Some of Christ's teachings concerning the Old Testament are as follows:

Do not think that I came to abolish the Law or the Prophets; I did not come to abolish, but to fulfill. For truly I say to you, until heaven and earth pass away, not the smallest letter or stroke shall pass away from the Law, until all has been accomplished (Matthew 5:17-18).

And He answered and said to them, "And why do you yourselves transgress the commandment of God for the sake of your tradition? For God said, 'Honor your   father and mother,' and, 'He who speaks evil of father or mother, let him be put to death' " (Matthew 15:3-4).

160

But regarding the resurrection of the dead, have you not read that which was spoken to you by God, saying, "I am the God of Abraham, and the God of Isaac, and the God of Jacob"? (Matthew 22:31-32).

He was also saying to them, "You nicely set aside the commandment of God in   order to keep your tradition. For Moses said, 'Honor your father and your mother'; and, 'He who speaks evil of father or mother, let him be put to death'; but you say, 'If a man says to his father or mother, anything of mine you might have been helped by is Corban (that is to say, given to God),' you no longer permit him to do anything for his father or his mother; thus invalidating the word of God by your tradition which you have handed down. . ." (Mark 7:9-13).

It is abundantly clear that Jesus considered the entire Old Testament (what the Jews of His day called "the Law and the Prophets") to be the inspired Word of God. He referred to the Old Testament authors as prophets (Matthew 11:13; 12:39; 22:40; 23:31-35; 24:15; 26:56; Luke 16:16-17, 31; 18:31; 24:44; John 6:45), meaning those who proclaim God's truth. In fact, Jesus spoke of the prophets as beginning with Abel and ending with Zechariah (Luke 11:49-51). This covers the exact time period of the Old Testament, from creation to about 400 bc. Since Christ is God Himself, His view of the Old Testament must be correct. Therefore, the Old Testament is the written Word of God.

Jesus Promised the New Testament would also be the Inerrant Word of God

Christ ascended to heaven before the New Testament was recorded. However, the promises He made to his apostles guaranteed that the New Testament would be the inspired Word of God:

Go therefore and make disciples of all nations, baptizing them in the name of the Father and the Son and the Holy Spirit, teaching them to observe all that I commanded you; and lo, I am with you always, even to the end of the age (Matthew 28:19-20).

Heaven and earth will pass away, but My words will not pass away (Mark 13:31).

But the Helper, the Holy Spirit, whom the Father will send in My name, He will teach you all things, and bring to your remembrance all that I said to you (John 14:26).

When the Helper comes, whom I will send to you from the Father, that is the Spirit of truth, who proceeds from the Father, He will bear witness of Me, and you will bear witness also, because you have been with Me from the beginning (John 15:26-27).

But when He, the Spirit of truth, comes, He will guide you into all the truth; for He will not speak on His own initiative, but whatever He hears, He will speak; and He will disclose to you what is to come (John 16:13).

But you shall receive power when the Holy Spirit has come upon you; and you shall be My witnesses both in Jerusalem, and in all Judea and Samaria, and even to the remotest part of the earth (Acts 1:8).

From these quotes of Christ, five conclusions can be drawn. First, Jesus promised that His teachings would be preserved. Second, He said that the Holy Spirit would remind the apostles of all that He told them. Third, the Holy Spirit would reveal future events to the apostles. Fourth, the Holy Spirit would guide the apostles into the truth (prevent them from promoting doctrinal errors). Fifth, the Holy Spirit would empower the apostles to be Christ's authoritative representatives to the world.

From the above conclusions it is clear that Christ promised to preserve His teachings through the apostles' writings.

Obviously, these writings make up the New Testament. Since Jesus is the almighty God, His plan cannot be thwarted. Therefore, since He promised to preserve His words through the teachings of the apostles, then their teachings (which have been passed on to future generations) are the teachings of Christ. Hence, they are the Word of God.

It should also be noted that Jesus taught that only the Old Testament and the teachings of His apostles (the New Testament) were the Word of God. The evidence declares Jesus to be God. Jesus taught that both the Old and New Testaments are the Word of God. Therefore, the Old and New Testaments are the Word of God.

Implications of the Bible being God's Word

Since the Bible can be shown to be God's Word, several implications follow. First, since the cosmological argument has shown God to be infinite and perfect, there can be no error in His Word as originally recorded. God can only proclaim truth; otherwise, He would be less than perfect. Therefore, the Bible is wholly true (inerrant). Second, since the Bible is God's inerrant Word, it is authoritative. God has spoken, and everything must be tested by the truth He has given. Third, whatever is taught in God's inerrant and authoritative Word should be adhered to by all. This work has already presented evidence for some of the major tenets of orthodox Christianity (the existence of one God, creation by God, the resurrection of Jesus, and Christ's deity). Since the evidence indicates the Bible is God's Word, whatever it teaches must be true. Therefore, other important Christian doctrines (e.g., salvation by grace through faith in Christ, the substitutionary death of Christ, the Trinity, and Christ's future return to earth) can be defended by showing that they are taught in the Bible.

Concerning salvation, the Bible teaches that all people are sinners who cannot save themselves (Romans 3:10, 23; 6:23;

Matthew 19:25-26). Scripture teaches that man cannot earn his salvation; salvation is a free gift given by God's grace (unmerited favor) to those who trust (believe) in Jesus for salvation (Ephesians 2:8-9; John 3:16-18; 6:35, 47; Romans 6:23). Only through Jesus can man be saved (John 14:6; Acts 4:12).

The Bible teaches that Jesus took mankind's punishment upon Himself by dying on the cross for our sins (Isaiah 53:5-6, 12; Matthew 1:21; Mark 10:45; John 1:29; Romans 5:8-10; Ephesians 1:7; 2 Corinthians 5:15, 21; 1 Timothy 2:4-6; Hebrews 10:10, 14; 1 Peter 2:24; 3:18; 1 John 1:7; 2:1-2; Revelation 5:9). The God of the Bible is holy and just; He cannot forgive sin unless it has been paid for in full. The good news is that Jesus (who is fully man and fully God) is the ultimately worthy sacrifice who has paid for the sins of the world through His death on the cross (Revelation 5:1-14). He died as a substitute for all of mankind. Those who accept Jesus as their Savior receive the salvation and forgiveness that He has purchased for them.

One of the most controversial teachings of Christianity is the doctrine of the Trinity, for this teaching transcends human understanding. This doctrine declares that the one true God eternally exists as three equal Persons (the Father, Son, and Holy Spirit). God is one in essence or nature (Mark 12:29; John 10:30), but three in Personhood (Matthew 3:16-17; John 14:16, 26; 15:26).

The Bible teaches that the Father is God (Galatians 1:1; 1 Peter 1:2). However, Jesus (the Son) is also called God and is described in ways that could only apply to God (Isaiah 9:6; Zechariah 14:5; John 1:1, 14; 5:17-18, 22-23; 8:58-59; 10:30-33; 17:5, 24; 20:28; Romans 9:5; Colossians 2:9; Titus 2:13; Hebrews 1:8; 2 Peter 1:1; 1 John 5:20; Revelation 1:17-18). Jesus is worshiped as God (Matthew 2:11; 28:9; John 9:38). The Holy Spirit is also called God (Acts 5:3-4; 1 Corinthians 3:16).

Some have speculated that the Father, Son, and Holy Spirit, since they are one God, must also be one Person, but, this is not what the Bible teaches. The Bible teaches that the Father, Son, and Holy Spirit are three distinct Persons (Isaiah 48:12-16; Psalm 110:1; Matthew 3:16-17; 28:19; John 14:16, 26; 15:26). Before anything was created, the three Persons of the Trinity communicated with each other (Genesis 1:26; 11:7), shared the glory of God (John 17:5), and loved each other (John 17:24). Even while Christ was on earth, He and the Father spoke to one another, thus proving they were not the same Person (Matthew 3:16-17; 26:39; Luke 23:46; John 17:1). When all the data is considered, it is clear that the Bible teaches that there is only one true God, but this God eternally exists as three equal Persons. Hence, the Bible teaches the doctrine of the Trinity.

The Bible also teaches that Jesus Christ will someday return to earth in power and glory. After His return, He will rule over the nations for one-thousand years (Matthew 24:29-31; Revelation 11:15; 19:11-16; 20:4-6). Since the available evidence declares the Bible to be God's Word, whatever it teaches must be true. Therefore, the biblical teachings concerning salvation, Christ's substitutionary death, the Trinity, and Christ's return should be accepted. It is also important to note that since whatever the Bible teaches is true, the morality taught in the Bible is authoritative. If God calls a practice wrong, then it is wrong, regardless of common political sentiment. Though the Bible student must differentiate between absolute moral laws which are universally binding on all men and temporary cultural laws prescribed for a specific people at a specific time, absolute moral laws taught in the Bible should be adhered to by all. The day will come when all must answer to God at the final judgment (2 Corinthians 5:10; Revelation 20:11-15).

ENDNOTES

1. Gary R. Habermas, *The Risen Jesus and Future Hope* (Lanham, MD: Rowman & Littlefield Publishers, 2003), vii.

2. Gary R. Habermas and Michael R. Licona, *The Case for the Resurrection of Jesus* (Grand Rapids: Kregel Publications, 2004), 48-75.

3. Ibid., 70-73.

4. J. P. Moreland, *Scaling the Secular City* (Grand Rapids: Baker Book House, 1987), 155-156.

5. Habermas and Licona, 98.

6. Gary R. Habermas, *The Historical Jesus* (Joplin: College Press, 1996), 152-157.

7. Moreland, 148.

8. Henry Thiessen, *Introduction to the New Testament* (Grand Rapids: William B. Eerdmans Publishing Company, 1987), 205.

9. John A. T. Robinson, *Redating the New Testament* (SCM Press, 1976), 54. Thiessen, 205. A. T. Robertson, *Word Pictures in the New Testament*, vol. 4. (Grand Rapids: Baker Book House, 1931), 16. D. A. Carson, Douglas J. Moo, and Leon Morris, *An Introduction to the New Testament* (Grand Rapids: Zondervan Publishing House, 1992), 283.

10. Habermas, *Historical Jesus*, 153-157.

11. Moreland, 150.

12. Habermas, *Historical Jesus*, 154.

13. Ibid., 154-155.

14. William Lane Craig, *Reasonable Faith* (Wheaton: Crossway Books, 1984), 285.

15. Gary R. Habermas and Antony Flew, *Did Jesus Rise From the Dead?* (San Francisco: Harper and Row Publishers, 1987), 58.

16. Ibid., 95.

17. Walter Martin, *Kingdom of the Cults* (Minneapolis: Bethany House Publishers, 1977), 86.

18. N. T. Wright, *The Resurrection of the Son of God* (Minneapolis: Fortress Press, 2003), 31, 147-148.

19. Ibid., 31.

20. Antony Flew, *There is a God* (New York: Harper Collins Publishers, 2007), 202-209.

21. Norman L. Geisler, ed. *Inerrancy* (Grand Rapids: Academie Books, 1980), 16-17.

Chapter Thirteen

Is Teaching Children
about God Child Abuse?

R ichard Dawkins asks the question, "Even without physical abduction, isn't it always a form of child abuse to label children as professors of beliefs that they are too young to have thought of?"[1] Hitchens concurs.

Richard Dawkins and Christopher Hitchens believe that teaching children about God is a form of child abuse. Since they would agree that child abuse should be outlawed, are these two militant atheists calling for the outlawing of Christian education, home schooling, and church Sunday school classes? Are they so intolerant that they want to outlaw the right of Christian parents to teach their children their faith? Do Dawkins and Hitchens believe that governments should force parents, churches, and Christian schools to teach atheistic evolution? If not, then why call the teaching of children about God "child abuse?" If yes, then Dawkins and Hitchens have exposed their extremely intolerant agenda—an agenda that seeks to abolish all speech contrary to that which promotes their own views.

In the name of tolerance, Dawkins, Hitchens, and their new, militant atheist buddies are promoting an intolerant agenda that would make Joseph Stalin proud. We must be clear on this—this is not an overstatement. Anyone who wishes to prohibit parents and private schools from teaching traditional religion to children is promoting tyranny, not tolerance. Apparently, the new atheists are only for freedom of speech when other people agree with them.

The new atheists consider themselves tolerant, but they can only tolerate those who agree with them. Traditionally, whenever a person can only tolerate those who agree with him, we have considered this intolerance, not tolerance. What makes the new atheists militant is that they are not content with intellectual discourse and debate—they want to stifle the voice of those who disagree with them. They are anti-free speech. They are intolerant—they want to force others to accept their views. They consider themselves free-thinkers, yet they want to deny others the freedom of thought.

Our founding fathers thought differently. The first amendment to the United Sates Constitution reads as follows: "Congress shall make no law respecting an establishment of religion, or prohibiting the free exercise thereof; or abridging the freedom of speech or of the press. . ." The founding fathers believed that God instituted human government to protect and defend a person's freedom of religion and freedom of speech, not to stifle it.

It was Karl Marx and Friedrich Engels, in *The Communist Manifesto*, who wanted to abolish religion and trample on freedom of speech. The agenda of the new atheists should have no place in a free society. If the new atheists have their way, the government will dictate what American citizens can believe, say, and teach. If the new atheists have their way, we will no longer be free. In a world without God, there can be no freedom. In a world without God, there can be no human rights. And this is the world that the new atheists seek to build.

The new atheists have embraced "the new tolerance." The traditional view of tolerance encouraged the freedom of religious expression and the freedom of speech. The Christian had the right to believe and proclaim that anyone who rejects Jesus as Savior will spend eternity in torment. The Muslim had the right to preach that only good Muslims will go to heaven. The traditional view of tolerance promoted dialogue between people who disagreed on religious, political, or moral issues. It upheld a person's right to disagree with others without fear of imprisonment or censorship; it respected the views of others even when they disagreed with your own beliefs.

The traditional view of tolerance has been replaced by a new definition of tolerance. In the name of tolerance, traditional beliefs are no longer tolerated. The goal of the new tolerance is not to get people to respect and tolerate the lifestyles and beliefs of all people. Instead, the goal of the new tolerance is to attempt to force everyone to "approve of and participate in" the attitudes and activities of the new morality. This new "tolerance" is rapidly becoming a religion of tolerance; however, it has the potential to be the most intolerant religion in the history of mankind. Those who choose to reject the new tolerance (also known as "the new morality" or "political correctness") are often "branded as narrow-minded bigots, fanatics, extremists, and hate-mongers and subjected to public humiliation and indoctrination."[2]

One of the members of my church worked for a large nationally known store chain. When he received his "diversity training," he was informed that he would not be allowed to greet customers by saying "God bless you" because this would be offensive to many people and infringe upon their rights. He was told he could read his Bible during his break time so long as he did not share his beliefs with other workers or customers. No such restrictions were placed upon his outspoken homosexual co-workers. This is a clear example of the new tolerance. Whereas the traditional view of tolerance promoted freedom of religion and freedom of speech, the new tolerance only allows for those freedoms if you are an adherent of the new tolerance. The new tolerance proclaims, "I am all for your freedoms of speech and religion so long as your share my views and my religion. Any other views are unacceptable and cannot be tolerated." The new tolerance is intolerant with a vengeance.

Unfortunately, this new tolerance is not limited to American soil. The United Nations, which may someday rule the world, also adheres to the new tolerance. The United Nations *Declaration of Principles on Tolerance* states that "Tolerance . . . involves the rejection of dogmatism and absolutism."[3] Obviously, this is a self-contradictory statement, for the rejection of dogmatism is itself a dogma, and the rejection of absolutism is itself an absolute.

In the name of the new tolerance, traditional Americans, in some cases, have been denied "schooling, scholarships, and employment."[4] In 1995, a US District judge from Texas "ruled that any student mentioning the name of Jesus in a graduation prayer would be sentenced to a six-month jail term."[5] It seems that anyone who holds to absolute standards (God's moral absolutes) will eventually lose their freedom of speech and be silenced so that politically-correct "progress" may continue.

The new atheists want to raise our children. Or, at least, they want an atheistic regime to raise and indoctrinate our children. But, the failed utopian dreams of the twentieth-century, and the dictatorships and genocides that followed, should be a lasting warning against the agenda of the new atheists. We have been down this road before. It is an ugly, bloody road that leads only to tyranny. It is a road we should not travel. The flight from the God of the Bible will always eventually lead to the prison camps of the Nazis or the Russian gulags. It will never lead to peace. Only in God can we have both peace with God and peace with man.

The new atheists claim that it is both irrational and harmful to believe in God. They claim that naturalism explains everything, and that belief in God is outdated and pre-scientific. They argue that teaching children about God is child abuse.

In this brief work, we have seen that it is not irrational to believe in God—there are good reasons to believe He exists. We have shown that it is not harmful to believe in the God of the Bible and that atheism has caused more death and suffering than aberrant versions of Christianity. We have exposed naturalism as a weak world view with poor explanatory power. And we have argued that

172

teaching children religion is not child abuse; it is freedom of speech.

When everything is said and done, God is not a delusion, and *true* religion does not poison everything. We seek joy, peace, and freedom in the world; but, these can only be found in God and His Son. We must pray for Richard Dawkins, Christopher Hitchens, and the new atheists. They long for joy and peace, but joy and peace will forever elude them, unless they bow before the God of the Bible. He is our joy; He is our peace. Apart from Him, we are nothing.

ENDNOTES

1. Richard Dawkins, *The God Delusion* (Boston: Houghton Mifflin Company, 2006), 315.

2. Josh McDowell and Bob Hostetler, *The New Tolerance* (Wheaton: Tyndale House Publishers, 1998), 32.

3. Ibid., 43.

4. Ibid., 32.

5. Ibid., 53.

Chapter 14

One Nation under Dawkins

Richard Dawkins and Christopher Hitchens believe that the world would be better off without belief in God. But, many other thinkers have disagreed with this assessment. Many thinkers have argued that if God is rejected, mankind will be worse off. In this chapter, we will look at three of these thinkers who paint a different picture of a world without God than the picture of the new atheists.

As the twentieth century comes to a close, we must properly diagnose the disease that has caused the unprecedented wars, bloodshed, and genocide which the past century has experienced. In this chapter we will discuss the prophetic insights of the German atheist Friedrich Nietzsche, as well as the prognostication of Christian thinkers C. S. Lewis and Francis Schaeffer, concerning the future of Western civilization. I will show that the nineteenth century's death of God has led to the twentieth century's death of both universal truth and absolute moral values, and that this in turn will lead to the death of man in the twenty-first century if the tide is not reversed.

Rather than creating a paradise on earth, the New Atheists, by rejecting God's moral absolutes, will produce a hell on earth. If Western Civilization continues its flight from God and ignores His moral absolutes, the foundations of society will crumble.

NIETZSCHE: PROPHET FOR THE 20TH CENTURY

Friedrich Nietzsche (1844-1900) proclaimed that "God is dead."[1] By this he meant that the Christian world view was no longer the dominant influence on the thought of Western culture. Nietzsche reasoned that mankind had once created God through wishful thinking, but the nineteenth century man intellectually matured to the point where he rejected God's existence.[2] Intellectuals throughout the world were embracing atheism as their world view, and the ideas of these intellectuals were beginning to influence the common people throughout Western civilization. According to Nietzsche, scientific and technological advances had made belief in God untenable.

But Nietzsche saw a contradiction in the thought of these intellectuals. Though he agreed with their atheism, he rejected their acceptance of traditional moral values. Nietzsche argued that, since God is dead, traditional values have died with Him.[3] If the God of the Bible does not exist, reasoned Nietzsche, then the moral values taught in the Bible should have no hold over mankind.

Nietzsche viewed existence as a struggle and redefined the good as "the will to power."[4] This was a logical outgrowth of his acceptance of the Darwinian doctrine of the survival of the fittest. Nietzsche called for a group of "supermen" to arise with the boldness to create their own values.[5] He proposed that, through their will to power, these "supermen" replace the "soft values" of Christianity with what he called "hard values." Nietzsche believed that the "soft values" of Christianity (self-control, sympathy, love for enemies, human equality, mercy, humility, dependence on God, etc.) were stifling human creativity and progress; these values encouraged mediocrity. But the "hard values" of the supermen (self-assertion, daring creativity, passion, total independence, desire for conquest, etc.) greatly enhance creativity.[6] Nietzsche considered the soft values a slave morality, and the hard values a master morality, and he promoted the latter.

Like the atheists of Nietzsche's day, the new atheists desire to dispose of God while clinging to some of the "soft values" of Christianity like compassion and tolerance. The new atheists seem oblivious to the fact that Darwinian evolution does not promote an ethic of compassion and tolerance. Instead, Darwinian evolution promotes survival of the fittest—toleration and compassion find no place in the bloody, cruel world of Darwinian evolution. While the new atheists claim they are tolerant and compassionate, they tend to support abortion, infanticide, and euthanasia. In some cases they and their colleagues seem to promote eugenics (for instance, ethicist Peter Singer). And, the new atheists imply they want to see the teaching of Christianity to children abolished by labeling it "child abuse."

The new atheists do not seem to appreciate the dependence of morality on God. They believe that Christianity can be stamped out without any drastic changes in the moral sphere. Nietzsche was not so naïve. He understood that the death of God meant the death of morality as well. Christianity battled and won the right for the new atheists to be heard. Yet, now that their voices are heard, the new atheists cry out against Christianity.

Nietzsche rejected the idea of universal, unchanging truths. He viewed truths as mere human creations, as metaphors mistaken for objective reality.[7] Therefore, Nietzsche showed that, since God is dead, universal truth, like absolute moral values, is dead as well.

Nietzsche predicted that the twentieth century man would come of age. By this he meant that the atheist of the twentieth century would realize the consequences of living in a world without God, for without God there are no absolute moral values. Man is free to play God and create his own morality. Because of this, prophesied Nietzsche, the twentieth century would be the bloodiest century in human history.[8] Still, Nietzsche was optimistic, for man could create his own meaning, truth, and morality. Set free from belief in a non-existent God, man could excel like never before. Nietzsche viewed the changes that would occur as man becoming more than man (the superman or overman), rather than man becoming less than man.

177

Nietzsche was the forerunner of postmodernism. A key aspect of modernism was its confidence that, through reason, man could find absolute truth and morality. Postmodernism rejects this confidence in human reason. All claims to having found absolute truth and morality are viewed by postmodernists as mere creations of the human mind.[9]

The history of the twentieth century has proven Nietzsche's basic thesis correct. Western culture's abandonment of the Christian world view has led to a denial of both universal truth and absolute moral values. The twentieth century has proven to be the bloodiest century in human history.[10] Hence, the Christian thinker must object to the optimism of Nietzsche. The death of God is not a step forward for man; it is a step backward—a dangerous step backward. If God is dead, then man is dead as well.

The comments of Roman Catholic philosopher Peter Kreeft are worth noting:

> One need not share Nietzsche's atheism to agree with his historical, not theological, dictum that "God is dead"—i.e., that faith in God is dead as a functional center for Western civilization, that we are now a planet detached from its sun. One need not share Nietzsche's refusal of morality and natural law to agree with his observation that Western man is increasingly denying morality and natural law; that we are well on our way to the Brave New World.[11]

C. S. LEWIS: THE ABOLITION OF MAN

The nineteenth century brought the death of God to Western culture. The twentieth century brought the death of truth and morality to Western culture. Two twentieth century Christian thinkers, C. S. Lewis (1898-1963) and Francis Schaeffer (1912-

1984), argued that the death of man will follow, unless of course man repents.

A Christian thinker should not be content with rightly analyzing and critiquing current ideas. A true thinker should also attempt to foresee the probable future consequences of ideas. In this way, a Christian thinker performs the role of a watchman by warning his listeners of future dangers (Ezekiel 33:1-9). C. S. Lewis and Francis Schaeffer had the courage to fulfill this role.

Lewis, in his prophetic work *The Abolition of Man*, critiqued an English textbook, written in the 1940's, which was designed for school children. Lewis found that more than English was being taught in this book, for the authors rejected objective truth and traditional values and proclaimed a type of moral relativism.[12] Lewis expressed concern for two reasons. First, the children who read this textbook would be easy prey to its false teachings.[13] Second, this would lead to a culture built on moral relativism and the rejection of objective truth, something that, according to Lewis, has not existed in the history of mankind.[14]

Lewis not only refuted the fallacious views of the authors, but also predicted the future consequences of this type of education. He argued that teaching of this sort would produce a race of "men without chests."[15] By this he meant men without consciences. According to Lewis, this would mean an entirely "new species" of man and "the abolition of man."[16]

Lewis argued that the practical result of such education would be "the destruction of the society which accepts it."[17] The rejection of all values leaves man free to recreate himself and his values.[18] When this power is placed into the hands of those who rule, their subjects will be totally at their mercy.

Lewis also saw in this rejection of traditional values a new purpose for science. In a sense, science is like magic in that both science and magic represent man's attempted "conquest of nature." However, science will become an instrument through which a few hundreds of men will rule billions of men,[19] for in man's conquest of nature, human nature will be the last aspect of nature to surrender to man.[20] Science will be used by future rulers to suppress the freedoms of the masses.

Lewis refers to the future rulers as "the man-moulders of the new age" or the "Conditioners."[21] It will be the job of the Conditioners to produce the rules, not to obey the rules.[22] The Conditioners (i.e., Nietzsche's supermen) will boldly create the laws the conditioned must obey. The role of education will become the production of artificial values which will serve the purposes of the Conditioners.[23] The Conditioners, through their Nietzschean "will to power" and motivated by the thirst to satisfy their own desires, will create their own new values and then force these "values" on the masses.[24]

According to Lewis, the rejection of traditional values and objective truth will lead to the same mentality in future rulers as that of "the Nazi rulers of Germany."[25] Traditional values will be replaced by the arbitrary wills of the few who rule over the billions,[26] and this will "abolish man" and bring about "the world of post-humanity."[27]

SCHAEFFER: THE POST-CHRISTIAN ERA & THE DEATH OF MAN

Francis Schaeffer proclaimed that Western culture is now in a "post-Christian era." By this he meant the same thing Nietzsche meant when he declared "God is dead." Schaeffer was saying that the Christian world view was no longer the dominant presupposition of Western culture. Now, a secular humanistic view of reality permeates the thought of the West.[28] Due to this change in world view, modern man has fallen below what Schaeffer called "the line of despair."[29] Schaeffer meant that, by throwing the God of the Bible out of the equation, modern man, left to himself and without divine revelation, could not find absolute truth and eventually gave up his search for it. According to Schaeffer, modern man no longer thinks in terms of antithesis (i.e., the law of non-contradiction); he now views truth as relative. And, since he believes there are no absolutes, modern man has rejected universal moral laws and has embraced moral relativism.

Schaeffer wrote concerning America, "our society now functions with no fixed ethics," and "a small group of people decide arbitrarily what, from their viewpoint, is for the good of society at that precise moment and they make it law."[30] Schaeffer compares this present climate of arbitrary lawmaking to the fall of the Roman Empire. The finite gods of Rome where not sufficient to give a base in law for moral absolutes; therefore, the Roman laws were lax and promoted self-interest rather than social harmony. This eventually led to a state of social anarchy as violence and promiscuity spread throughout the empire. To keep order, the Roman Empire had to become increasingly more authoritative. Due to Rome's oppressive control over its people, few Romans believed their culture was worth saving when the barbarian invasions began.[31] Schaeffer saw that America, like ancient Rome, had turned to arbitrary laws which have led to an increase in crime and promiscuity, which in turn has led to ever-increasing government control. Schaeffer stated this principle as follows:

The humanists push for "freedom," but having no Christian consensus to contain it, that "freedom" leads to chaos or to slavery under the state (or under an elite). Humanism, with its lack of any final base for values or law, always leads to chaos. It then naturally leads to some form of authoritarianism to control the chaos. Having produced the sickness, humanism gives more of the same kind of medicine for the cure. With its mistaken concept of final reality, it has no intrinsic reason to be interested in the individual, the human being.[32]

Schaeffer also noted that most American leaders no longer consider themselves subject to God's laws. They often view themselves as answerable to no one. They do not acknowledge "inalienable rights" given to each individual by God. Instead, American leaders play God by distributing "rights" to individuals and by making their own arbitrary laws. Schaeffer quotes William Penn who said, "If we are not governed by God, then we will be ruled by tyrants."[33]

Schaeffer saw the 1973 legalization of abortion as a by-product of man playing God by legislating arbitrary laws and by the few forcing their will on the many.[34] But, according to Schaeffer, this is just the beginning, for once human life has been devalued at one stage (i.e., the pre-birth stage), then no human life is safe. Abortion will lead to infanticide (the murdering of babies already born) and euthanasia (so called "mercy-killing").[35] Christianity teaches that human life is sacred because man was created in God's image, but now that modern man has rejected the Christian world view (the death of God), the death of man will follow (unless modern man repents) and man will be treated as non-man. Schaeffer documents the erosion of respect for human life in the statements of Nobel Prize winners Watson and Crick. These two scientists, after winning the Nobel Prize for cracking the genetic code, publicly recommended that we should terminate the lives of infants, three days old and younger, if they do not meet our expectations.[36]

In his response to behavioral scientist B. F. Skinner's book *Beyond Freedom and Dignity*, Schaeffer argued that Western culture's rejection of God, truth, and God's moral laws will lead to the death of man. Written in 1971, Skinner's book proposed a "utopian" society ruled by a small group of intellectual elitists who control the environment and genetic makeup of the masses. Schaeffer stated, "We are on the verge of the largest revolution the world has ever known-the control and shaping of men through the abuse of genetic knowledge, and chemical and psychological conditioning."[37] Schaeffer referred to Skinner's utopian proposals as "the death of man,"[38] and wrote concerning Skinner's low view of C. S. Lewis:

Twice Skinner specifically attacked C. S. Lewis. Why? Because he is a Christian and writes in the tradition of the literatures of freedom and dignity. You will notice that he does not attack the evangelical church, probably because he doesn't think it's a threat to him. Unhappily, he is largely right about this. Many of us are too sleepy to be a threat in the battle of tomorrow. But he understands that a man like C. S. Lewis, who writes literature which stirs men, is indeed a threat.[39]

Schaeffer understood not only the failure of secular humanism, but he also realized that Eastern pantheism offered no escape from the death of man. Only a return to the Christian world view could save the West from the death of man. He stated:

Society can have no stability on this Eastern world-view or its present Western   counterpart. It just does not work. And so one finds a gravitation toward some form of authoritarian government, an individual tyrant or group of tyrants who   takes the reins of power and rule. And the freedoms, the sorts of freedoms we have enjoyed in the West, are lost. We are, then, brought back to our starting   point. The inhumanities and the growing loss of freedoms in the West are the result of a world-view which has no place for "people." Modern humanistic materialism is an impersonal system. The East is no different. Both begin and end   with impersonality.[40]

Schaeffer called upon evangelicals to sound the alarm, warning the church and society to repent, for the death of man is approaching:

Learning from the mistakes of the past, let us raise a testimony that may still turn both   the   churches   and   society around-for the salvation of souls, the building of   God's   people, and at least the slowing down of the slide toward a totally humanistic society and an authoritarian suppressive state.[41]

The Twentieth-First-Century—A World without God

Nietzsche wrote that Western culture's rejection of God would inevitably lead to the rejection of absolute truth and universal moral values. Allan Bloom confirmed that this has indeed been the case when he began his epic book *The Closing of the American Mind* with these words: "There is something a professor can be absolutely certain of: almost every student entering the university believes, or says he believes, that truth is relative."[42] Still, Nietzsche wrongly believed that this rejection of truth and morality would improve humanity by ushering in the "overman."

Lewis and Schaeffer agreed with Nietzsche's death of God, truth, and morality hypothesis, but, since they were Christians, they argued that this would not be a step forward for man. Instead, this would bring about the death of man. Though I believe that Lewis overstated his case by asserting that the death of man would create a "new species," I agree that, apart from Western culture's repentance, some type of death of man is inevitable. Man is presently being treated as non-man throughout the world (i.e., abortion, infanticide, euthanasia, religious persecution, genocide, violent crimes, etc.), and this trend will continue to increase apart from a return to the Christian world view.

As I see it, the death of man will involve spiritual, social, and psychological aspects. The death of man will be characterized by man being further alienated from God (the lost becoming harder to reach with the Gospel), from others (mankind becoming more and more depersonalized), and from himself (the light of man's moral conscience and his thirst for God will be dimmed). People, especially those in positions of authority, will treat other people as less than human. Man's love for man will grow cold.

To prevent, or at least slow down, the death of man, Christian thinkers must defend the reality of God, absolute truth, absolute moral values, as well as the dignity of man and the sanctity of human life. Still, we must do more than refute current ideologies; we must also proclaim to a complacent church and world where those ideas will take us in the twenty-first century if we refuse to repent. Like Lewis and Schaeffer, we must resist the temptation to pick dates for Christ's return or dogmatically declare that these are the last days, for we do not see the future with certainty—maybe Western culture will repent. Therefore, like

Lewis, Schaeffer, and the Old Testament prophets, we must call our culture to repent. We must tell our generation that the nineteenth century gave us the death of God, and the twentieth century gave us the death of truth and morality. Without widespread repentance, the twenty-first century will bring the death of man. Just as the removal of God from our schools has all but destroyed our public school system, the removal of God from the reigning ideas of Western culture will surely destroy our civilization. The death of God will ultimately lead to the death of man, if we do not turn back to the God of the Bible. Unless trends are reversed and the Christian world view is restored as the dominant perspective in Western culture, the twenty-first century will surpass the twentieth century in tyranny, violence, and ungodliness.

Our founding fathers believed that "all men are created equal." They did not mean that all men share the same talents or have the same potential. They meant that all men and women were created in the image of God. Therefore, all men are equal in God's eyes and deserve equal rights and freedoms. Our founding fathers believed that God instituted human government to protect the God-given rights of each individual. Because these rights were given to men by God they were called "unalienable rights." Governments were to protect these rights; they did not have the authority to take these rights from men. Rights such as life, liberty, and the pursuit of happiness were God-given. What God has given, reasoned the founders of this great country, let no man take away.

The belief that God created man formed the basis for the political/economic experiment called the United States of America. No people in the history of human government have enjoyed greater freedom than the fortunate citizens of this land. Still, the foundation for this freedom has been slowly deteriorating for several generations. The doctrine of atheistic evolution has replaced the belief in God as Creator. The political and economic implications are clear. For, if man was created by God, then the equal rights of all citizens should be protected. However, if there is no God and if we evolved from apes, then men are not equal. Some of us are probably "more evolved" than others. Maybe the "more

185

evolved" ones (they would probably rather be called the "enlightened ones" or "brights") should make the decisions for the less fortunate people. In short, creation by God implies human equality, while evolution encourages a "survival of the fittest" mentality. Darwinian evolution encourages the idea that not all people have evolved equally, and the less-evolved (or the less-enlightened ones) should not be able to reproduce at the rate of the enlightened ones. The founder of Planned Parenthood, Margaret Sanger, promoted eugenics, as did the Nazis. Both Sanger and the Nazis claimed Darwinian evolution as the justification for their views.

If America is to return to its former status as the land of the free, its people will have to recover their lost belief in God as Creator. This belief must not be a mere verbal acknowledgement of God as Creator, but a conviction that effects the way we Americans think and act. Until that day comes, our freedoms will continue to dwindle.

Our founding fathers acknowledged God as the Creator. They believed that His laws were above all human governments. God's moral laws were seen as eternal and unchanging. They were absolute standards to which both citizens and leaders had to submit. The laws of this nation were not based upon the arbitrary and changing decisions of man; instead, they were established by the unchanging nature of the Almighty God. Even the government itself had to adhere to the commands of the Supreme Being.

Unfortunately, the intellectual climate has changed drastically in this country. A secular view of government has replaced the traditional idea of a God-ordained government. This secular view recognizes no God above human government—there are no divine laws that exist above the government; hence, the government is not accountable to God. The government has become the ultimate now that God (the real ultimate Being) is ignored. When the government rejects God, the government replaces God; it becomes an authoritarian state. This was the way things went in the Soviet Union and Red China. This is also the direction that Richard Dawkins, Christopher Hitchens, and their militant atheist colleagues will take us—despite their claims to be tolerant.

Without acknowledging God as above our government, can we remain free? Can we expect to be treated with dignity and respect if our leaders no longer see us as beings created by God and in His image? Once God is taken out of the equation, the government begins to play God. Government officials become answerable to no one since the government itself becomes the highest authority. No power will be recognized above the government. Arbitrary laws will be created which declare things to be right or wrong merely because the government has deemed them as such. Whatever jeopardizes the power of those in authority will be deemed illegal; whatever furthers the agenda of those in positions of power will be declared legal. The rulers will replace education with politically-correct indoctrination (in fact, this is already going on in America's public schools) to ensure they stay in power.

If someone responds by saying that things can never get this bad in America, then this person only shows his or her ignorance concerning the horrors of human history and the sinfulness of mankind. As Lord Acton once said, "Power corrupts, and absolute power corrupts absolutely." Our founding fathers echoed this sentiment as they limited the power of our leaders. We must learn the lessons that history teaches its future generations. We must accept the fact that *any attempt to establish a free society is doomed to failure if God's laws are not acknowledged as being above the government itself.*

The vast majority of Americans (about 94%) still believe that God exists. They have rejected philosophical atheism (the denial of God's existence). Still, most Americans have embraced practical atheism—they live like no God exists. We must no longer pay mere lip service to God. If we, as a culture, genuinely believe that God exists, then we must live consistently with that belief.

America must return to the God who blessed her so abundantly. She must recognize that there is always a Stalin or a Hitler behind the curtain, waiting to be revealed. America is not immune to the disease of tyranny. It can infest any nation. If the United States government does not submit itself once again to God's unchanging laws, there will be no freedom. For, without the recognition of God as the supreme Lawgiver, there can be no freedom. God is essential to human freedom.

If Dawkins and the new atheists have their way, the government will recognize no authority above itself. Man's unalienable rights will be ignored. The sanctity of human life will be rejected by those in positions of power. We are already seeing our country move in this direction. We have witnessed the murder of over 50 million unborn babies through abortion. We can no longer be called one nation under God. Now infanticide and euthanasia are becoming more common in America.

If the new atheist agenda succeeds, we will see the censorship of anyone who opposes their Darwinian beliefs. Eventually, the eugenics program of past evolutionists may be restarted. It is true that Dawkins himself might not see the consequences of his view. But, one nation under Dawkins will be a nation where the undesirables will be exterminated, Christianity is abolished, and freedom of speech is stifled. If America accepts Dawkins' advice, we will be a nation void of freedom. And, where there is no freedom, there is only tyranny. The new atheists set out to free mankind from the chains of religion. Instead, their views will bind us in the chains of tyranny.

ENDNOTES

1. Friedrich Nietzsche, *The Portable Nietzsche*, ed. Walter Kaufman (New York: Penguin Books, 1968), 124, 447.

2. Ibid., 143, 198.

3. Norman L. Geisler and Paul D. Feinberg, *Introduction to Philosophy* (Grand Rapids: Baker Book House, 1980), 408.

4. *The Portable Nietzsche*, 570.

5. Geisler and Feinberg, 408.

6. Ian P. McGreal, ed. *Great Thinkers of the Western World* (New York: HarperCollins Publishers, 1992), 409-410.

7. *Portable Nietzsche*, 46-47.

8. Frederick Copleston, A *History of Philosophy*, vol. VII (New York: Doubleday, 1963), 405-406.

9. Stanley J. Grenz, *A Primer on Postmodernism* (Grand Rapids: William B. Eerdmans Publishing Co., 1996), 83.

10. R. J. Rummel, *Death by Government* (New Brunswick: Transaction Publishers, 1997), 9. Rummel estimates that, in the twentieth century alone, between 170 and 360 million people have been killed by their own governments during times of peace. (This does not include the millions of unborn babies who were aborted in this century.)

11. Peter Kreeft, *C. S. Lewis for the Third Millennium* (San Francisco: Ignatius Press, 1994), 107.

12. C. S. Lewis, *The Abolition of Man* (New York: Collier Books, 1947), 23.

13. Ibid., 16-17.

14. Ibid., 28-29.

15. Ibid., 34.

16. Ibid., 77.

17. Ibid., 39.

18. Ibid., 62-63.

19. Ibid., 69, 71.

20. Ibid., 72.

21. Ibid., 73-74.

22. Ibid., 74.

23. Ibid.

24. Ibid., 78, 84.

25. Ibid., 85.

26. Ibid.

27. Ibid., 85-86.

28. Francis Schaeffer, *A Christian Manifesto* (Westchester: Crossway Books, 1981), 17-18.

29. Francis Schaeffer, *The Complete Works of Francis A. Schaeffer*, vol. I (Westchester: Crossway Books, 1982), 8-11.

30. Schaeffer, *A Christian Manifesto*, 48.

31. Schaeffer, *Complete Works*, vol. V, 85-89.

32. Schaeffer, *A Christian Manifesto*, 29-30.

33. Ibid., 32-34.

34. Ibid., 49.

35. Schaeffer, *Complete Works*, vol. V, 317. see also vol. IV, 374.

36. Ibid., vol. V, 319-320.

37. Ibid., vol. I, 381.

38. Ibid., 383.

39. Ibid., 382-383.

40. Ibid., vol. V, 381.

41. Ibid., vol. IV, 364.

42. Allan Bloom, *The Closing of the American Mind* (New York: Simon & Schuster, 1987), 25.

Chapter 15

Conclusion: A Quick Review

We have responded to the new atheist's objections to belief in God and Christianity. We will close this discussion by summarizing this material in question and answer format. Brief answers will be given to key questions that deal with the arguments of the new atheists. It is my hope that this chapter will be a quick reference for all who desire to respond to the arguments of the new atheism.

1) Is it Irrational to Believe in God?

We have shown that the charge of the new atheists that it is irrational to believe in God is simply not true. There are good reasons to believe in God. In fact, I believe it is more reasonable to believe in God than it is to be an atheist. Belief in God is a more reasonable way to explain the evidence of human experience than is atheism. The origin of the universe, the continuing existence of the universe, the design and order in the universe, and the existence of universal moral laws make more sense in a theistic universe. Belief in God offers a better explanation than does atheism for common aspects of human experience such as meaning in life, human free will, human rights, our experience of guilt, self-awareness, and our hope that evil will be defeated. Belief in God is rational—there is good evidence to believe in God (see Chapter Four).

2) Is it Harmful to Believe in God?

The new atheists blame all of mankind's problems on belief in God. But, this is not the case, for the damage done by atheistic regimes far outweighs the damage done by so-called Christian cultures. Studies show that the atheistic, communistic regimes of the Soviet Union and Red China have murdered more of their own people (over eighty million) during peace time than all the people who have died in mankind's wars throughout history! The Nazis combined neo-pagan beliefs with an acceptance of Darwinian evolution. The short history of the Third Reich produced a death toll of over twenty million. All the damage done by professing Christians throughout two-thousand years of history does not come close to the carnage produced by atheistic and neo-pagan regimes influenced by Darwinian evolution. Any evil done by professing Christians is still evil. But, the evil done in the name of Christ does not come close to the evil done in the name of Darwinian evolution. It is much more harmful for cultures to embrace atheism than it is for cultures to accept belief in God (see Chapter Five).

3) Does Naturalism Explain Everything?

Naturalism is the belief that only natural causes exist— there are no supernatural causes. Hence, there is no God and miracles are impossible. However, by limiting all explanations to natural causes, naturalism is a reductionist position. It oversimplifies the issues. For, there is no adequate natural explanation for love, truth, and goodness. In fact, nearly all scientists agree that the universe had a beginning (i.e., the Big Bang Model). But, the universe is all of nature. Hence, all of nature needs a cause. Therefore, the cause of all of nature cannot be natural—we have run out of natural causes. The cause of the universe (all of nature) must transcend nature—the cause must therefore be supernatural (see chapters three and four).

4) Has Darwinism Disproved God?

There are several reasons why Darwinism has not disproved the existence of God. First, when Darwin wrote *The Origin of Species* in 1859, he still believed in the existence of God. Second, if evolution really occurred, then it still needs God to bring something from nothing, life from non-life, multi-celled animals from single-celled animals, etc. For, all these "evolutionary" jumps violate or transcend natural laws. Hence, a superseding of natural laws is needed. But, when the laws of nature are superseded, we call this a miracle. Therefore, even if evolution is true, it still needs God to design the universe and bring intelligence from non-intelligence. Natural causes do not explain the origin of the universe, first life, and complex life forms. If evolution is true, it needs God. But, if God exists, then He did not have to use evolution. He could have created the universe and man without using evolution. Whatever the case, Darwinian evolution has not disproved God as claimed by the new atheists. Third, it is debatable as to whether Darwinian evolution has itself been proven (see Chapter Three).

5) Is God Essential to Freedom?

The belief that man was created in God's image is the only firm protection of human rights. America's founding fathers believed all people were created equal, and that each human has unalienable rights given to him by God. Once we remove God from the equation, there is no real basis for human rights. Man is mere molecules in motion, an accidental product of chance and time. Man is a mere animal. Governments that have refused to recognize God have generally had less respect for human life and rights. Also, human governments that refuse to acknowledge God's existence recognize no authority over themselves. Government officials that do not recognize God often put themselves in the place of God. Governments that acknowledge God recognize God as the ultimate authority. This offers a further protection to human life. When belief in God is rejected by the leaders of a nation, tyranny eventually follows (see chapters five, thirteen, and fourteen).

6) Is Man an Animal?

Atheists like Peter Singer, Christopher Hitchens, and Richard Dawkins believe that man is merely an animal. Christians disagree. Christians believe that human life is infinite in value since God created man in His own image. If we reject belief in God, then man is merely an animal. This is why Peter Singer is the leading proponent of animal rights. But, even this is inconsistent with atheism. For, if there is no God, then not only is man's worth devalued, but so also is the value of animals. Hence, if there is no God, then men are mere molecules in motion. Animals are also mere molecules in motion. Humans have no more value than a mound of dirt. If atheistic evolution is true and man is an animal, then man has no value. This explains why atheistic regimes do not respect human life and human rights. The Christian belief that man is not an animal but was created in God's image is the only safeguard to human rights and the sanctity of human life (see Chapter Fourteen).

7) Is Teaching Children about God Child Abuse?

Teaching children about God is not child abuse—it is called freedom of religion. Forcing parents to have their children indoctrinated in atheistic evolution is child abuse and censorship. This was practiced by the Soviet Union and Red China. Atheistic indoctrination of children should not be practiced in America. The parents should determine what their children are taught, not the all-powerful state. When the state controls education, education becomes indoctrination in political correctness. The children are not taught what is best for them to know. Instead, they are taught what those in power want them to believe in order to protect the positions of those in power (see chapters thirteen and fourteen).

8) Have Professing Christians Committed Atrocities in the Past?

Yes, professing Christians have committed atrocities in the past such as the inquisition and persecution of "witches." Sin is sin even when committed by professing Christians. Several things need to be noted. First, not all professing Christians are genuine Christians (Matthew 7:21-23). Second, the Bible teaches that even true Christians continue to sin (1 John 1:8-10). Third, the new atheists greatly exaggerate the number of innocent people killed in the name of Christianity. Fourth, the new atheists minimize or ignore the well over one-hundred million people murdered in the name of atheism and neo-paganism in the twentieth century. Fifth, the Crusades began as a defensive act by Christian nations that were being invaded by Muslim warriors. Every nation has the right to defend itself and its allies. Even when Christians do not practice what they preach, this in no way disproves Christianity (see Chapter Five).

9) Can Atheists Be Moral?

Yes, atheists can be moral—they can make excellent, peaceful neighbors. They can make good moral choices. The Bible teaches that all humans were created in God's image and that we have God's moral laws written in our hearts (Genesis 1:26-27; Romans 2:14-15). Still, no man can please God in his own strength. Jesus is the only way to the Father; He is the only way we can be saved (John 14:6; 3:16-18). But, atheists can be moral citizens in the eyes of men; but, this is because both atheists and Christians were created in God's image.

10) Can Atheists Invent Their Own Moral Laws?

Yes, atheists can invent their own moral law or code. This is because God has written His moral laws on our hearts and in our consciences (Romans 2:14-15). When atheists produce their own moral laws, this does not disprove Christianity. It merely shows that Christianity is true, that a moral God created man in His image. Hence, all humans are moral beings. Still, many of us stifle the voice of God in our consciences more than others do.

11) Did Morality Evolve Into Existence?

It is very unlikely that absolute, universal moral laws evolved into existence from physical things like dirt or water. It is highly unlikely (I believe it is impossible) that morality would, by chance, evolve from non-moral "stuff." This is why most atheists reject absolute moral laws. However, it seems self-evident to most people that raping people or torturing innocent babies is evil for all people, at all times, in all places. If atheistic evolution cannot produce absolute moral laws, then it fails to explain this important aspect of human existence. The new atheists have no moral foundation from which to condemn rape or torture; yet, they stand in moral judgment on the God of the Bible. Therefore, the new atheists are not consistent atheists. Consistent atheists are moral relativists; yet, moral relativists cannot live consistently with their moral relativism. We all live like there are moral absolutes (see chapters four and seven).

12) Did Reason Evolve Into Existence?

If human reason has a non-rational cause, can we trust it? If reason evolved by chance from matter then there would be no way for us to know it really works. There would be no way to know that reason really does enable us to know truth. The new atheists use their reason to attempt to disprove God; but, they do not realize that this presupposes that human reason has a rational cause (i.e., the rational God). If we were created by a rational God in His image (i.e., as rational beings), and if this God created the universe in a way suitable for us knowing truth about it, then human reason can be trusted to help us find truth. If, on the other hand, we evolved from mindless matter, then, even if human reason evolved, there would be no guarantee that reason works. We would have no basis to trust our reason. But the case is even worse than this for the new atheists. For, it is highly unlikely (I would argue it is impossible) that human reason evolved from mindless matter by chance. Human reason needs a rational cause. Finite human reason needs an infinite rational Cause to fully explain its existence and validity. Reason did not evolve into existence (see Chapter Four).

13) Did Self-Awareness Evolve into Existence?

The new atheists believe that self-awareness evolved into existence by chance. But, this is clearly absurd. There is no way one could receive human self-awareness through matter, chance, time, and purely natural causes. It seems that the only probable explanation is that the self-aware God created human beings in His image so that we are also self-aware. Self-awareness did not evolve from primordial soup (see Chapter Four).

14) Can an All-Good God Allow Evil and Human Suffering?

The existence of evil and innocent human suffering is not inconsistent with the existence of an all-good, all-powerful God. God allows evil for the purpose of a greater good. God did not create evil—He created the possibility of evil. We call this possibility of evil human and angelic free will. Fallen humans and fallen angels actualized the existence of evil by freely rebelling against God. Hence, evil is a privation—a lack of a good that should be there. God created everything that exists. Everything that exists was good when God first created it. But, when humans and angels used their free will to oppose God, we perverted and corrupted God's perfect creation.

The continuing existence of evil does not rule out the possibility of God's existence. Since an all-good God has the power to destroy or defeat evil, He allows evil to continue to exist for purposes of a higher good. Though God's ways and thoughts are as far above our ways and thoughts as the heavens are above the earth (Isaiah 55:8-9), and we will never have Him totally figured out, we can sometimes see why He allows specific cases of evil. God often uses evil to bring others to Himself. We often grow spiritually in the midst of suffering and trials (James 1:2). Without evil there would be no such thing as courage, or the ability to love our enemies. For, without evil there would be no evil entities to fear and, without evil, there would be no enemies—everyone would be our friend. There are certain goods that God could not actualize without allowing evil to exist. An all-good, all-powerful God can co-exist with evil and human suffering; but, since He is all-good, He will use that evil for purposes of a greater good (see Chapter Six).

15) Are Miracles Possible?

The new atheists assume that miracles are impossible— they have not disproven miracles. They fail to understand that science primarily deals with repeatable processes of the present. Science deals with natural processes. But, a miracle, by definition, is a supernatural act. If the God of the Bible exists, then miracles are possible. This is because God is the one who established the laws of nature—the usual way things occur in nature. He is not bound by the laws of nature; He can choose to intervene by superseding the laws of nature whenever He chooses to do so. In other words, if God exists, then miracles are possible. Natural laws do not prescribe the way things must be; they describe the way things generally occur. Natural laws do not a priori rule out the possibility of miracles. In this work, we have provided the reader with good reasons to believe that God exists. Therefore, miracles are possible. Individual miracles claims must be investigated and tested on their own merit. When someone investigates the resurrection of Jesus from the dead, the evidence indicates that Jesus did in fact rise from the dead (see chapters eight and twelve).

16) Is the Old Testament God an Evil God?

The new atheists repeatedly condemn the God of the Old Testament as an evil God. There are several ways we can respond to this accusation. First, what moral standard do the new atheists appeal to in order to condemn God? Atheism has no absolute moral law. Second, the new atheists interpret numerous Old Testament passages in novel ways in order to make their case. Apparently, they ignore Old Testament scholarship and choose to interpret the passages in ways that aid their case for atheism. Third, the Old Testament God (who happens to also be the God of the New Testament—the one true God) is not evil—He is the source of all that is good. Fourth, the Old Testament God often uses evil to bring about purposes of a greater good. And fifth, the Old Testament God had to go to extreme means to protect His chosen nation (Israel) since she would be entrusted with God's written revelation and the coming Savior of the world. God is not a racist—He blessed Israel so that she would be a blessing to all nations. For, salvation comes from Israel. If God did not protect Israel and minimize the influence of her pagan neighbors, then Gentiles would still be lost—no one would be saved. For the Jewish Messiah is the hope of the nations; the Messiah of Israel is the Savior of the world. If God allowed marriage between Jews and pagan Canaanites to be common, then the Jewish religion (which was revealed to them by the true God) would be lost to mankind. We would have no way of knowing the true God. Finally, as the giver of life, only God has the right to take life. He is sovereign over life. To protect Israel, her identity and revealed religion, God ordered the Jews to wipe out their Canaanite enemies. This was not the norm for the Old or New Testament. But, apparently it was necessary to preserve the Jewish nation and the one true faith so that Jew and Gentile could be saved through the sacrifice of Jesus. God is just and His judgment is fierce; still, God is gracious and merciful. He has provided salvation for mankind through His chosen nation.

17) Does the Bible Contain Contradictions?

The new atheists claim that the Bible is filled with contradictions. But, this is not the case. Any claim to supposed contradictions in the Bible can be refuted in several ways. First, Christians do not claim that copies of the Bible are inerrant. We only claim that the original manuscripts were without error. Hence, there are mistakes in the copies. Second, the atheist might be misinterpreting the passages under consideration. Third, figurative language might be mistaken for literal language (or vice versa). Fourth, a speech or sermon found in the Bible could have been paraphrased or abridged by the biblical authors. Therefore, the wording in one Gospel may differ from the wording in another Gospel. Fifth, the biblical authors may have rounded off the numbers before recording some event.

18) Do Theists Bear the Burden of Proof?

The new atheists claim that, since they merely lack belief in God, they do not share the burden of proof with theists. But, this is not the case. The new atheists have their own world view (i.e., view of reality). They therefore share the same burden of proof that the theist bears. Also, since only four percent of Americans are atheists, the new atheists at least bear the burden of explaining why over ninety percent of Americans disagree with them. Why are ninety percent of Americans wrong and the new atheists right?

19) Are Atheists More Charitable than Christians?

New atheists like Sam Harris imply that Christians or other religious people are no more charitable than atheists. Though it is true that many professing Christians do not practice what they preach, recent research indicates that Americans of faith are much more likely to donate to charities than atheists or agnostics.[1]

20) Is Atheism on the Rise?

The new atheists believe that atheism is on the rise. They believe that more and more people are becoming atheists, and that the percentage of atheists in the world is growing. However, this is not the case. Recent research shows that currently only four percent of Americans consider themselves to be atheists.[2] Though the percentage of non-religious people is growing in America, these people do not claim to be atheists. They believe in the existence of some type of God, but do not feel led to affiliate with any organized religion. Still, the percentage of atheists in America, and throughout the world, is not growing. This is interesting due to the fact that atheists have gained control of the schools, education, and the media. Yet, the percentage of atheists remains the same. Even in Russia, a nation whose people were indoctrinated in atheistic evolution under the former Soviet Union, the percentage of atheists is low and remains low.[3] Atheism is not on the rise. However, biblical Christianity does appear to be on the decline in Western nations, though it is on the rise in southern African nations, Eastern nations, and Central and South American nations.

But, the fact remains that atheism has never been a widespread belief in any culture, even if that culture was governed by atheist leaders.

21) Are There Good Reasons to Believe Christianity is True?

In this work we have shown that there are good reasons to believe that Christianity is true. This is despite the claim made by the new atheists that belief in God is irrational. There is better evidence for the reliability of the New Testament manuscripts than for any other ancient writings. If someone rejects the historical evidence for New Testament reliability and is consistent with that rejection, then he would have to reject the historical reliability of all other ancient writings—he would have to be skeptical concerning all of ancient history! But, this would be absurd. Also, there is excellent historical evidence that Jesus clearly claimed to be God and Savior on numerous occasions, and that He bodily rose from the dead to prove He is God and Savior (see chapters ten, eleven, and twelve).

22) Are Christians biased?

The new atheists, like many non-Christians claim that Christians are biased towards God and miracles when they read the Bible. It is implied that, if Christians were more open-minded, they would see that the miraculous events of the Bible never really occurred. I agree that Christians have biases before they begin their research; but, the same can be said for the new atheists. All humans are biased. The new atheists are biased against the possibility of miracles. Hence, when they read the Bible, they automatically reject the miraculous events as mythological.

Everyone is biased. The question is not: are you biased? Instead, the question should be: whatever it is that you are biased about, is it true? Is there good evidence for your biases? Therefore, both the Christian and the non-Christian are biased. There is no such thing as a person without biases or presuppositions. But, we must put our biases and our presuppositions to the test to see if we are justified in accepting them.

23) Who Designed God?

Richard Dawkins mistakenly believes that he refutes the argument for God's existence by merely asking the question: Who designed God? Unfortunately, this only reveals Dawkins' lack of philosophical sophistication, for his question totally misses the point. The traditional arguments for God's existence show that there cannot be an infinite regress of causes and effects, nor can there be an effect without a cause. Hence, the traditional arguments for God, especially the teleological (the argument from design) and the cosmological (the argument from the contingency of the universe) show that the ultimate Cause of all the finite, temporal, changing beings must be an infinite, eternal, unchanging Being. In other words, the ultimate Cause of the universe must be an uncaused Cause, and the ultimate Designer of the universe must be an eternal, undersigned Designer (see Chapter Three).

24) Does the Cause have to be More Improbable than the Effect?

Again, Richard Dawkins misses the point when he asserts that the Cause (i.e., God) has to be more improbable than the effect (i.e., the universe). One wonders where Dawkins learned his philosophy. The existence of human life on the planet earth is only improbable if it got here by chance. If it was created by God, then the existence of human life is not improbable at all—it was planned and designed by an infinitely wise God. Dawkins totally misunderstands the argument for God from design. The design argument merely asserts that human life coming into existence by chance is so improbable that it is more reasonable to believe that it did not get here by chance—it was designed.

ENDNOTES

1. Gary R. Habermas, "The Plight of the New Atheism: A Critique" *Journal of the Evangelical Theological Society*, vol. 51, No. 4, December, 2008. Habermas refers to the 2007 research of the Barna Group.
2. Rodney Stark, *What Americans Really Believe*. (Waco: Baylor University Press, 2008), 117-119.
3. Ibid., 118.

About the Author

Dr. Phil Fernandes is the president of the Institute of Biblical Defense, which he founded in 1990 to teach Christians how to defend the Christian Faith. He is also the pastor of Trinity Bible Fellowship in Bremerton, Washington, and teaches apologetics and philosophy for Columbia Evangelical Seminary and the Imago Dei Institute. He also teaches Bible and Philosophy at King's West School in Bremerton, WA. Fernandes has earned the following degrees: a Ph.D. in Philosophy of Religion from Greenwich University, a Master of Arts in Religion from Liberty University (where he studied apologetics under Dr. Gary Habermas), and a Master of Theology degree from Columbia Evangelical Seminary. He is currently doing Doctor of Ministry studies in apologetics under Dr. Norman Geisler at Southern Evangelical Seminary. Fernandes has publicly debated leading atheists in defense of Christianity at colleges and universities such as Princeton and the University of North Carolina (Chapel Hill). Fernandes is a member of four professional societies: the Evangelical Theological Society, the Evangelical Philosophical Society, the International Society of Christian Apologetics, and the Society of Christian Philosophers. He has authored several books: *The God Who Sits Enthroned: Evidence for God's Existence, No Other Gods: A Defense of Biblical Christianity, Theism vs. Atheism: The Internet Debate* (co-authored with leading atheist Dr. Michael Martin), *God Government, and the Road to Tyranny: A Christian View of Government and Morality*, and *Contend Earnestly for the Faith: A Survey of Christian Apologetics*.

Over 1,000 audio lectures, sermons, and debates by Dr. Fernandes can be downloaded for free from his websites philfernandes.com and biblicaldefense.org. His sermons, lectures, and debates have been downloaded over two million times in more than eighty countries throughout the world. If you would like Dr. Fernandes to speak at your school or church, please contact him at tbf@sinclair.net.

CPSIA information can be obtained at www.ICGtesting.com
Printed in the USA
BVOW070636020512

289166BV00002B/8/P